Equipped
to Lead

Library of Congress Cataloging-in-Publication Data

Equipped to lead : children's Sunday School guide.
    p. cm.
  Includes bibliographical references.
  ISBN 978-0-88177-542-6
  1. Christian education of children. I. Discipleship Resources
BV1475.3.E68 2008
268'.432--dc22

                          2008030578

Equipped to Lead

Children's Sunday School Guide

The Consultative Group on Ministry among Children

DISCIPLESHIP RESOURCES

PO BOX 340003 • NASHVILLE, TN 37203-0003

www.discipleshipresources.org

Equipped to Lead is offered as training material by the Consultative Group of Ministry among Children (CGMC), a network of Churches Together in Britain and Ireland.

Churches and organizations currently represented on CGMC

Baptist Union of Great Britain
BRF
Christian Education
Church of England
Church of Ireland
Church of Scotland
Church in Wales
Congregational Federation
Council for Sunday Schools and Christian Education in Wales
Christian Education Association Scotland
The Methodist Church in Great Britain
Methodist Church in Ireland
The Moravian Church
Presbyterian Church of Wales
Quaker Home Service
Roman Catholic Church
Roots for Churches
The Salvation Army
Sunday School Society for Ireland
United Reformed Church
Welsh National Centre for Religious Education
International Christian College

Organizations working with CGMC through personal membership

The Church Lads' and Church Girls' Brigade
CPAS
Scripture Union
South Yorkshire Ecumenical Training Group

Acknowledgment

CGMC wishes to thank all those involved with the project, either with the writing or the field-testing of material, and is grateful for their ideas, inspiration and hard work, which have enabled this publication to evolve from its predecessor, *Kaleidoscope*, into new, exciting and vibrant training material.

Particular thanks go to Rosemary Johnston and Steve Pearce for acting as coordinators for the project, to Roger Walton for guiding the initial steps, and to Sue Doggett and BRF for understanding, encouragement and gentle guidance along the way.

We also extend a special thank you to the Westhill Endowment for their generous support for the writing, launching and ongoing development of this project.

From the Writing Group

The production of the *Equipped to Lead: Sunday School Teacher's Guide* (*Equipped*) material has been a creative ecumenical journey.

For some time, a variety of basic courses had been produced to encourage and equip those working with children in the church. Then, through the Consultative Group on Ministry among Children (CGMC), a group was set up to produce the first ecumenical training material. *Kaleidoscope—Training material for those working with children in the church* was published in 1993 and has been hugely successful. More than 15,000 copies have been sold and many more people have enjoyed training locally with others from a wide variety of churches. It has been translated into Welsh, and the Swedish translation was used ecumenically by the Baptist, Methodist and Swedish Mission Covenant Churches in Sweden.

However, there is a growing awareness of changes in the context for children's ministry. Insights about children's spiritual development and learning, as well as exploration of fresh approaches to worship and community participation, have led to the need for new material.

Denominations are now making more overt their expectation that those entrusted with the well-being of children should be appropriately trained. At the same time, the government is working on outlining a common core of skills for children's workers, which may become mandatory, and churches are keen that the training undertaken by their children's workers should be seen as compatible with that initiative.

After agreeing that a new set of ecumenical material could build on the work done and take advantage of new developments, CGMC set up a group to enable the project. All denominations in membership of Churches Together in Britain and Ireland were invited to send representatives to a residential meeting to seek a way forward. The resulting working group had representatives from Wales, Scotland, Ireland and England. From this sprang the principles, aims, objectives, writing groups, editorial meetings, pilot groups and, finally, the completed material.

A year's collaborative work led to the six sessions presented here, alongside its supporting website, and the opportunity to gather a portfolio to give evidence of learning. A constant thread through the journey has been an ecumenical generosity, sharing ideas, time and talent.

Important Information

Photocopying permission

The right to photocopy material in *Equipped to Lead* is granted for the pages that contain the photocopying clause: "Reproduced with permission from *Equipped to Lead* published by Discipleship Resources 2008," so long as reproduction is for use in a teaching situation by the original purchaser. The right to photocopy material is not granted for anyone other than the original purchaser without written permission from Discipleship Resources.

Contents

Foreword

Children's ministry is a vital element of the churches' work. As the church seeks to be faithful in its mission, it must also seek to provide for those children in its midst and strive for the best that can be offered. *Equipped to Lead* is another important step forward in ensuring that we offer the best resources and leadership we can to the children with whom we have contact.

It is particularly beneficial that we have common material to encourage local churches in their thinking and action. The benefits of working collaboratively, as we continue to discover, are enormous. Encouraging our children to grow into God's image as they tell stories, share ideas, explore the Bible and seek inspiration from the Holy Spirit is central to these materials.

We are pleased to commend this new focus for encouraging the development, skills and knowledge of those engaged in ministry with children. As they respond to the ongoing challenge of enabling children to be a full part of the community of the church, we should commit ourselves to the prayerful support of those working with children in all our names.

Bob Fyffe, General Secretary, Churches Together in Britain and Ireland

Introduction

Guiding Principles

All children are made in the image of God. They are loved unconditionally by God and were affirmed in the life and ministry of Jesus. This is reflected in the Christian community, where:

- God's love is made real through human life and relationships.
- All children and adults are of equal value.
- The Holy Spirit speaks powerfully through children as well as adults.
- Everyone experiences enjoyment, safety and encouragement in belonging.
- All contribute and all receive, learning from each other.
- The Bible is accessible to all.
- All respect one another as people of faith.
- Differences are acknowledged and diversity celebrated.
- All are being changed by the love of Christ and share the good news in the wider community.
- Worship, celebration and encountering God are vital to the growth of faith.
- All have a sense of belonging to the universal Church and of serving the world together.

Rights of the Child

The UN Convention on the Rights of the Child has been an important document for all those working with children, both in and out of the Church. Its main drives are reflected through *Equipped*, which are as follows.

- Calling for the provision of specific resources, skills and contributions necessary to ensure the survival and development of children to their maximum capability.
- Requiring the creation of means to protect children from neglect, exploitation and abuse.
- When adults are making decisions that affect children, children have the right to say what they think should happen and have their opinions taken into account, while recognizing that the level of a child's participation in decisions must be appropriate to the child's level of maturity.

Safeguarding and Child Protection

We do not include a separate training module for the protection of children and youth in *Equipped to Lead*. We recommend that each congregation study *Safe Sanctuaries,* by Joy Thornburg Melton, and use this material to train all workers with children and youth. Many churches, conferences, and judicatories have adopted the Safe Sanctuaries guidelines and training. Melton is a Christian educator and an attorney whose ministry concerning reducing the risk of child abuse.

Training with the *Safe Sanctuaries* material helps create a safe environment and awareness among those who work with children.

Safe Sanctuaries is published by Discipleship Resources. In addition to the basic resource book, a DVD is also available.

Aims and Learning Outcomes

Aim One

To help participants to develop an understanding of children and the skills required to nurture children in their journey of faith.

Learning Outcomes

- To experience and understand the process of how people develop, learn and grow in faith.
- To listen to and accompany children as partners in faith.
- To evaluate their own skills, gifts, strengths and weaknesses and identify a plan for personal development.
- To help children engage with the Bible as a part of the living, personal and ongoing story.
- To work creatively with children, using a variety of methods to suit different learning styles.
- To develop skills to encourage children in expressing and valuing their spirituality and making their own response of faith.
- To share resources and ideas.

Aim Two

To provide the participants with the opportunity to explore and reflect on their own experience of faith and Christian journey, and the effect it has on their work with children.

Learning Outcomes

- To recognize the need to feel valued, equipped and supported in their role.
- To reflect on and share their own faith story.
- To develop a reflective, enquiring approach to the Bible and its use in faith and life.
- To explore their experience of worship, celebration and spiritual life.
- To recognize the role of, and raise their awareness of, children's ministry.
- To develop the skills and habit of reflecting on their work with children.

Aim Three

To help participants capture and share a vision of a Christian community in which children's faith is expressed and valued.

Learning Outcomes

- To articulate an understanding of God's call to be a pilgrim people, a missionary community and a global family.
- To advocate the active participation of children in mission and ministry.
- To explore ways of working with children in a variety of contexts, including new expressions of church.

Using *Equipped*

This material is planned for ease of use in a variety of ways. As the material has been written from a number of ecumenical settings, it is hoped that it will be delivered ecumenically wherever possible.

Each of the six sessions is designed to stand alone. It would make sense to do them in the order suggested, but it is possible for an individual or group to select one session and then perhaps add others at a future date. This could happen occasionally over time; alternatively, all the sessions could be tackled in a regular pattern of one per week, fortnight or month. Once a week would give less time for reflection and putting ideas into practice, so a longer gap is recommended. A wider spread of time gives the opportunity to add visiting places of interest as well as exploring the web links.

Each session is designed to take two hours. This timespan will be achieved by selecting from the material available. Each session could be extended to cover a whole day by using more of the material, adding some from the website and slowing the pace in items used, to allow more discussion, exploration and activity. Instead of allotting specific timings to each activity, which will rarely reflect the actual experience of every group using the material, "hammer" indicators have been used instead.

- ⚙ One hammer indicates a simple introductory activity that might take only a short time to complete.
- ⚙ Two hammers indicate a more in-depth activity that will require some thought and time.
- ⚙ Three hammers indicate a high-content section containing the main thrust of the teaching.

By choosing more of the one-hammer activities and fewer of the three-hammer ones, you will have a shorter session. The reverse, of course, will give a longer session.

A session is laid out as follows.

- ⚙ **Aim** of the whole module.
- ⚙ **Learning Outcomes** that should be achieved through the session.
- ⚙ **Materials Needed** to run the session.
- ⚙ **Opening Thought** to enable reflection.
- ⚙ **Starters:** ways into the topic.
- ⚙ **Core:** the main teaching element.
- ⚙ **Biblical Thought,** tying the teaching to the Bible.
- ⚙ **Reflection on Learning:** a prompt to help better understanding of the session.
- ⚙ **Worship:** suggestions to close the session in themed worship.
- ⚙ **Personal Reflection Sheet** to assist participants in noting their learning outcomes.
- ⚙ **Portfolio Checklist** for those wishing to collect evidence of learning.

The Personal Reflection sheet can be completed by the participant at home or at the end of the session. It is intended to enable the answering of the following questions.

- ⚙ What encouragements, concerns and challenges have this module raised for you?
- ⚙ What would you like to explore further?
- ⚙ What action will you take or encourage your church community to take as a result of this module?
- ⚙ What will be the benefits for the children in your group and for your church community?
- ⚙ Which aspects of this session can you talk about and check out with the children in your group?

For those who want to use *Equipped* as part of an accredited learning course, the portfolio checklist summarizes the learning for which you would need to show proof, in order to satisfy the requirements.

Safeguarding and Child Protection

Title of your denomination's policy document:

What do you do if you have an issue relating to child protection?

Who is the person in your church who deals with child protection issues?

What permission and registration forms do you complete when a new child joins the group?

What training in child protection have you had?

If none, when is the next available training?

When is the next review of your local child protection procedures?

Reproduced with permission from *Equipped to Lead* published by Discipleship Resources © 2008

Introductory Session

Aim

To provide a basic introduction to working with children in a church context.

Learning Outcomes

- To share hopes and fears about working with children.
- To reflect critically on a variety of strategies for developing relationships with children.
- To evaluate the use of a code of conduct.
- To explore issues around children, theology and culture.
- To consider how to approach a session with children.
- To determine future learning needs.

Materials Needed

Before the Session

✔ Labels or name badges for people as they arrive

Starters

✔ Flipchart paper and pens
✔ An apple
✔ Post-it® notes

Core

✔ Copies of "Children and Church Questionnaire" (see page 22)
✔ Copies of "Assessing Training Needs Questionnaire" (see page 23)

Are not two sparrows sold for a penny? Yet not one of them will fall to the ground unperceived by your Father. And even the hairs of your head are all counted. So do not be afraid; you are of more value than many sparrows. (Matthew 10:29–31, NRSV)

Our role in working among children for the church involves being God's representative in communicating God's love and care. That love and care are also shown to children by the way we act towards one another as adults. In this learning session, the group will not count the hairs on each member's head, but will develop a better understanding of one another's role in children's ministry.

Starters

Who am I?

You will need:
- ✔ Flipchart paper and pens

In threes, check that you know one another's names, then find out about the context of one another's children's work. Talk about:

- ◉ How you each feel half an hour before a session begins.
- ◉ Your hopes and concerns about working with children and young people.

There will be feedback only on the hopes and concerns, which should be written on flipchart paper.

In the whole group, feed back your hopes and concerns and write them on flipchart paper. Then discuss the hopes and concerns that the children may be bringing to the groups with which the participants are involved. Write them up on the flipchart too, and compare this list with the first.

Think about how to find out how children are really feeling. Why is it important to find out?

Apple consequences

You will need:
- ✔ An apple

Take the apple and start off a story about it: for example, "This apple came from a small orchard not far from here, and one day . . ." Pass the apple to someone else in the group, who must continue the story, using the word "apple" in his or her contribution to the story.

Pass it around the whole group so that everyone contributes, and continue until the story is complete.

Why am I here?

You will need:
- ✔ A flip chart or large sheet of paper, and pens
- ✔ Post-it® notes

How many ways can this question be answered? Write as many as you like, one on each Post-it® note. It is up to individuals how they interpret the question. Stick the responses onto a flipchart, without comment.

Join up with one or two other people and talk more specifically about why each person is here in this group. Come back into the whole group and talk about the experiences of this activity.

- ◉ How did different people interpret the question?
- ◉ How did people feel during the Post-it® exercise?
- ◉ What insights does this exercise give into working with children?

Core

Children and Their Culture

Any adult who wants to work with children needs to understand a little about what it is like to be a child in today's world. The way an adult sees the world is quite different from the way a child sees it. An adult leader can never be a child, but can make some effort to get inside the world of children.

There are many important and powerful influences on children, and the values that are strongly communicated through the media are significant and formative. Spending time on children's websites and reading magazines aimed at children are a good investment and give pause for thought.

Look at a selection of children's magazines. Skim-read them to get a feel of the impact and tone of the publication. As you read:

- Ask yourself what is the message being given there about school/home/lifestyle/spirituality/young women.
- List any words or phrases you don't recognize.
- Identify one or two articles that you would like to share with the rest of the group.
- Note the main themes of the advertising.

Share your findings with the rest of the group. If there is time together, try putting the values that children observe and experience in the media alongside those communicated explicitly and/or implicitly by the church, and see the differences. Make two lists and ask:

- Which culture is easier to understand?
- How easy is it to be part of both?
- How easy is it to make choices within each culture?
- If the church is "counter cultural", what does that mean?

The world of children and how children develop are explored further in Session 1.

Children and Church _____

> You will need:
>
> ✔ Copies of the "Children and Church Questionnaire" (see page 22)

Individually, complete the "Children and Church Questionnaire" and then share responses together. How far are these statements true of the church you attend? (Mark 0 for "Not true at all" and 5 for "This is clearly our church's belief and practice.")

Approaching a Session _____

Share the experience of a memorable session you have led with children, one you have seen led, or one you experienced as a child. What worked well and why did you remember it?

What challenges have you met, or are you anticipating, in your work with children? Compile a list of these challenges under the following headings:

- Starting a session
- Using time in a session
- Working with a whole group
- Choosing activities
- Working with other leaders

The following thoughts may start off your discussion.

Starting a Session

Think about how the tone is set in the first five minutes (atmosphere, layout, welcome and so on). How can you start the session off to build relationships with the children?

Using Time in a Session

When planning, always build in time to engage with a group and individual children. Consider the fact that one-to-one conversation is usually easier when a child is engaged in a practical task, especially a low-key task.

Working with a Whole Group

Use "circle time" techniques from time to time. With younger children, a "show and tell" can be an important, regular part of the session. For older children, frequent positive affirmation games will build up the group's capacity to relate positively and share more deeply.

Choosing Activities

Always plan to spend time on what is important, and avoid giving time to activities that benefit the adults more than the children. For example, if you meet on a Sunday morning, avoid a weekly commitment to "producing" something that has to be performed for the adults in church.

Working with Other Leaders

Consider how you plan and review together.

Assessing Training Needs

> You will need:
>
> ✔ Copies of the "Assessing Training Needs Questionnaire" (see page 23)

This session has drawn attention to just some of the skills and knowledge that are important for any adult working with children on behalf of the church. Some of this skill comes with experience, but only if you take time to do some conscious learning as well, and also take time to reflect critically on your experiences. Many church denominations have recognized the six sessions of this training as the basic training requirement for children's workers. Look at the outline of these sessions on the "Assessing Training Needs Questionnaire" and fill in the boxes to help you assess which topics are priorities for you.

Biblical Thought

Children and Church

Split into three groups, each group looking at one of these Bible passages: Psalm 78:1–8; Matthew 18:1–5; Luke 13:34–35.

If this was the only passage in the Bible you read, what would your "theology" (your understanding of God's view) of children be? Try to sum it up in three statements, and briefly sum up how this would affect the life of the whole church. What do you feel now about the way you would work with children in your church, and why?

In the whole group, consider the different "theologies" that different church traditions have, and the different ideas there are about why children are in the church. You may recognize the following models.

- ⚙ If the children are considered to be the church of tomorrow and will only become useful disciples when they become adult members, the provision for children may be aimed at keeping them in contact with the church so that their real learning and work can begin when the time comes.

- ⚙ If the children are seen as the church of tomorrow but need to lead a Christian life now, the children's work may be seen as a schooling in the Christian life. The children's activities may work on the assumption that the faith must be learned and a Christian way of life followed. Information giving and Bible teaching will aim to lead to a vibrant adult faith and spiritual life.

If children are seen as being as much a part of today's church as the rest of the congregation, and equally valuable members, then it will be vital that children's provision in the church is of a high quality, aimed at equipping their ministry. Children will be enabled to take part in all aspects of church life.

If someone came into your church and tried to guess what your theology of children was by watching the life of the church, what conclusions do you think they would draw? Think about visiting another church and guessing what their theology of children might be.

Reflection on Learning

Building Relationships with Children_____

What is the group's observations of how they have all worked together so far?

Every group has some principles about how the relationships in the group will work—between children, between adults, and between children and adults. Some of those principles will be explicit (having quiet periods to listen to others, keeping one another safe by not running around, and so on) and some implicit (how children address adults, how the children are involved in decision making, and so on).

In a new group, in an established group meeting for the first time after a break, or in a group with lots of new members, it may be good to work together to produce a code of conduct and agree on it. The process for doing this will be important: perhaps there will be some suggestions from both adults and children, followed by a voting procedure to decide

which ones are to be included. Read the following examples and share your responses to them.

Rules Set by the Leaders

Don't run.
Don't shout.
Don't answer back.
When the leader is talking, listen.
Have fun!

Rules Compiled by the Children

Welcome to our club. We hope you have a good time, but when you are here you need to do things in our club way. We don't like anyone teasing people, because we are all friends. Don't bring any treats or chocolate just for you! We like playing silly games and running around, but when the leaders tell us to stop, we STOP! You'll probably find out that we are all a bit (lot!) noisy and talk too much. But we need to remember that when one of the leaders is telling us what to do, we shut up and listen. And we need to listen to one another as well.

We have one word that is banned—BORING. And we don't use any swear words at all. We have drinks every week so you don't need to bring your own. Finally, at the end of the night, no one goes home until someone comes to pick him or her up.

We hope you have a good time at our club.

Rules Agreed to by Everyone

Be nice.
Help others.
Do the activities when the leaders ask us to.
Make new friends.
Help new people.
Enjoy ourselves.
Listen carefully.
Walk.
Join in.
Don't hit or kick people.
Don't refuse to join in.

Don't be mean.
Don't run around the room.
Don't talk when someone else is talking.
Don't leave the club room.

How would you go about working with your group to agree to a "code of conduct"?

Worship

Read 1 Corinthians 12:4–6. As a focal point, have a selection of apples used in different ways: apple juice, apple pies, caramel apples and so on. Take time while listening to some music to consider the gifts and talents that you have in relation to children's ministry, because we all have a concern for children and can offer our different skills in different ways. Finish this meditation with a prayer together.

Suggested Song

The Lord is good to me
and so I thank the Lord
for giving me the things I need,
the sun and the rain and the apple seed.
The Lord is good to me.

And every seed that grows
will grow into a tree,
and one day soon there will be apples there
for everyone in the world to share.
The Lord is good to me.

"Johnny Appleseed":
www.scoutingresources.org.uk/song_song05.html

At the close of the session, invite everyone to share in the variety of apple products together, in celebration of their involvement in children's ministry.

Children and Church Questionnaire

Mark 0 for "Not true at all" and 5 for "This is clearly our church's belief and practice".

1. Children are considered important in our church. 0 1 2 3 4 5

2. People in our church feel comfortable with children. 0 1 2 3 4 5

3. Children in our church are happy to be there. 0 1 2 3 4 5

4. People in our church are willing to support children's work by praying. 0 1 2 3 4 5

5. People in our church are keen to see children involved in worship throughout the year. 0 1 2 3 4 5

6. Children are encouraged to join in with other church activities as well as worship. 0 1 2 3 4 5

7. The adults in our church talk to the children and know their names. 0 1 2 3 4 5

8. When the children enter the church, they are ignored, but someone greets their parents. 0 1 2 3 4 5

9. We want children in our church to keep the church going in the future. 0 1 2 3 4 5

10. There is evidence around the building of the children's involvement in church life. 0 1 2 3 4 5

11. Our church wants our children to see that God loves them and has a purpose for their lives. 0 1 2 3 4 5

12. Our church wants children to become active members of the church today. 0 1 2 3 4 5

13. We want children to be able to look back, later in life, with warm affection at what church meant to them. 0 1 2 3 4 5

Reproduced with permission from *Equipped to Lead* published by Discipleship Resources © 2008

Assessing Training Needs Questionnaire

No knowledge: **N**   Some knowledge: **S**   Fully confident: **F**

Session 1: Child Development

- To understand how children develop physically, emotionally, intellectually, socially, morally and spiritually. ☐
- To appreciate the range of learning styles and approaches that there can be within a group. ☐
- To reflect on personal experience of life and faith, and the effects of this on ways of working with children. ☐
- To consider work with children in the light of some theories of human development. ☐

Session 2: Leadership Skills

- To evaluate current skills, gifts, strengths and weaknesses and identify possibilities for personal development. ☐
- To recognize the need to feel valued, equipped and supported in their role. ☐
- To develop the skills and habit of reflecting on their work with children. ☐

Session 3: Program Planning

- To understand how learning styles in childhood differ, and are influenced by society and culture. ☐
- To work creatively with children, using a variety of learning styles. ☐
- To plan original sessions and deliver published programs to meet the needs of children. ☐
- To develop the practice of reflecting on and evaluating sessions. ☐

Session 4: Children and Community

- To reflect on stories from different contexts and distill principles of good practice. ☐
- To develop strategies for developing new areas of work with children in a variety of contexts. ☐
- To explore an understanding of what it means to be "church". ☐
- To advocate the active participation of children in mission and ministry. ☐

Session 5: Pastoral Awareness

- To share insights about a variety of pastoral issues. ☐
- To explore how power is used in working with children. ☐
- To identify issues involved in providing a safe environment, physically, emotionally and spiritually, for children. ☐

Session 6: Spirituality and the Bible

- To explore the meaning of "spirituality" and its relationship with faith. ☐
- To gain an understanding of ways in which the Bible can enrich prayer and spiritual activities. ☐
- To experience a time of spiritual reflection. ☐
- To develop an awareness of the different styles of prayer that may be used, both in community worship activities and personal communication with God. ☐

Reproduced with permission from *Equipped to Lead* published by Discipleship Resources © 2008

SESSION ONE
Child Development

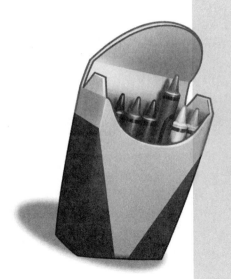

Aim

To reflect on and extend understanding of how children develop, and to apply this understanding to interaction with children.

Learning Outcomes

⚙ To understand how children develop physically, emotionally, intellectually, socially, morally and spiritually.

⚙ To appreciate the range of learning styles and approaches that there can be within a group.

⚙ To reflect on personal experience of life and faith, and the effects of this experience on our ways of working with children.

⚙ To consider work with children in the light of some theories of human development.

Materials Needed

Starters

✔ Flipchart
✔ Large sheets of paper and pens
✔ 8½ x 11 sheets of paper

Core

✔ Large sheets of paper and pens
✔ "Child Development" charts photocopied from pages 33–37
✔ "Images of Faith" sheet photocopied from page 38

Worship

✔ Photographs of children (cut from newspapers and magazines) showing different ages/races/abilities, different contexts, different emotions
✔ A table on which to spread out the pictures so that everyone can move around to look at them

The child Jesus grew. He became strong and wise, and God blessed him.
(Luke 2:40, CEV)

Starters

Then and Now

> **You will need:**
> ✔ Two large sheets of paper and at least two pens per group

In groups of three or four, talk about the "When You Were Seven" questions below, and collect the answers on one of the large sheets of paper. Enjoy sharing responses.

When You Were Seven

1. What was your favorite food?
2. What was your favorite toy or game?
3. What was your favorite story?
4. What was your favorite TV or radio program?
5. Did you know any Christians?
6. What did you know about Christianity and Christian faith?
7. Did you feel part of a church? Why/why not?

Now work through the "Now They Are Seven" questions below, thinking particularly of the children known to the group members. Record the answers on the other large sheet of paper.

Now They Are Seven

1. What foods are popular with seven-year-olds today?
2. What toys and games do they play with?
3. What sorts of stories do they like?
4. What TV programs are the most popular with this age group?
5. Do the children in your group know any Christians other than you?
6. What do they know about Christianity and Christian faith?
7. Do they feel part of your church? Why/why not?

Display the completed sheets. Everyone look at the answers of other groups. Are there any surprises? Any shocks? Any challenges? What are the implications of all this for work with children?

Alternatively, you can adapt the questions to relate to different age groups, focusing on five-year-olds or ten-year-olds, for example.

Different Approaches

> **You will need:**
> ✔ An 8½ x 11 sheet of paper for each person

The task is to make a paper cup using only an 8½ x 11 sheet of paper. After ten minutes, or sooner if everyone has finished or given up, look at the results of everyone's efforts.

- How many different designs are there?
- Can they all be described as cups?
- How did you approach the challenge? (Trial and error? Distant memories of doing it in the past? Copying someone else? Working together?)
- Would you have felt more (or less) comfortable if you had been given printed instructions, or if someone had demonstrated how the task should be carried out?
- What does this show you about yourself and about one another?
- How would the children in your group have approached this challenge?
- To what extent does your preferred way of learning affect the way you work with your group?

For more information on learning styles, see Session 3, pages 57–60.

Core

How Children Grow and Develop

You will need:

✔ Large sheets of paper and pens
✔ "Child Development" charts, photocopied from pages 33–37

Join up with two or three others who work with the same age group of children that you work with. Picture a child or children of this age. On a large sheet of paper, draw the outline of a child and write on the main characteristics of the age group. Think about all aspects of a child's being: physical, social, emotional, spiritual and intellectual. When finished, compare and contrast your diagram with the "Child Development" charts.

⚙ Do the charts help you to understand better how children develop? Why/why not?
⚙ To what extent are they relevant to children with special needs?
⚙ What insights has this exercise given into understanding the children you work with?

Every child is an individual. Some are gifted and talented in particular ways. Others have special needs of one sort or another, be they mental, physical, or emotional. No two children develop in exactly the same way or at the same rate, and there can be wide variations among children of the same age. The differences in how children develop raise many questions for children's work, including these:

⚙ Which methods and activities are most appropriate for the age range?
⚙ To what extent do you use them?
⚙ What are the implications for working with a mixed age range?
⚙ What are the dangers of expecting too much or too little of the children you work with? Which of these two "traps" do you find it harder to avoid?

Talk about these questions. What other questions occur to you?

Motivation and Needs

According to Abraham Maslow, an American psychologist, we all have a range of needs, as illustrated in the diagram below. Our most basic needs are at the bottom. Each layer of needs must be met before the next layer can be attended to. So, for example, a person will not be able to feel that they belong if their physical needs and safety needs have not yet been met. When our needs have been met at one level, we are able to move on to the next. If we have unmet needs at lower levels, we are unlikely to be motivated to learn for learning's sake.

The child psychologist Mia Kellmer Pringle, on the other hand, has identified the following needs as being significant in the development of children and young people.

⚙ The need for love and security
⚙ The need for new experiences
⚙ The need for praise and recognition
⚙ The need for responsibility

How do these theories relate to your work with children? To what extent do they help you to understand any problems you have had in working with children?

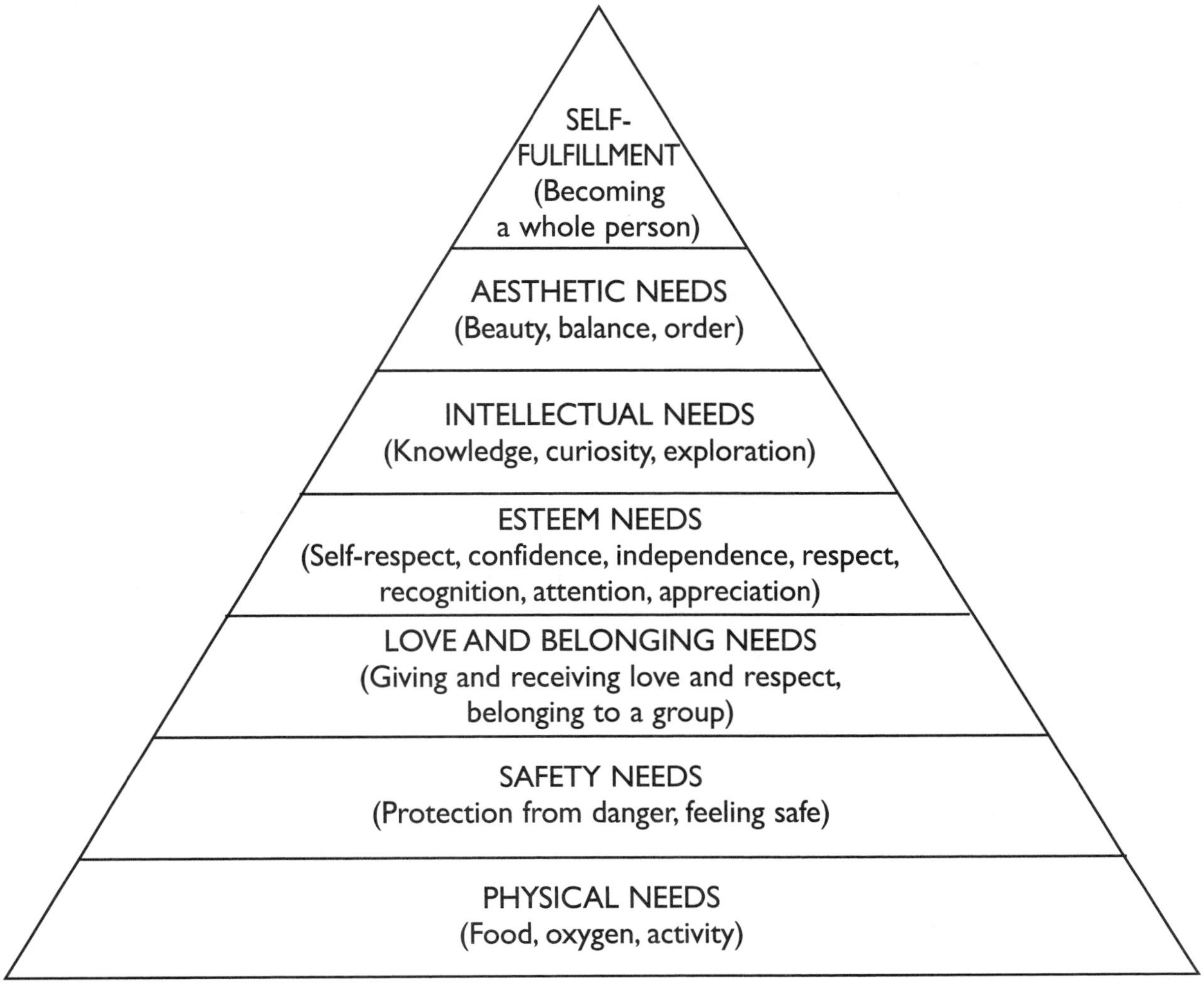
SELF-FULFILLMENT
(Becoming a whole person)
AESTHETIC NEEDS
(Beauty, balance, order)
INTELLECTUAL NEEDS
(Knowledge, curiosity, exploration)
ESTEEM NEEDS
(Self-respect, confidence, independence, respect, recognition, attention, appreciation)
LOVE AND BELONGING NEEDS
(Giving and receiving love and respect, belonging to a group)
SAFETY NEEDS
(Protection from danger, feeling safe)
PHYSICAL NEEDS
(Food, oxygen, activity)

Focus on Faith

You will need:

- ✔ A flipchart or large sheet of paper, pens and pencils
- ✔ "Images of faith" sheet, photocopied from page 38

Suggest ways to complete the phrase "Faith is . . . " For example, could it be said that faith is . . .

- . . . a seed to be planted and nurtured?
- . . . a spring of water needing to be channeled?
- . . . a quantity of knowledge to be crammed into people's heads?

Look at the "Images of faith" sheet. Reflect individually on what each image says about faith and the journey through life. Which one "speaks" most clearly? Is there another image that would illustrate your experience better? If so, draw it in the empty box on the sheet.

Those who wish to share may talk to a partner about why she or he has chosen a particular image, and in what way it represents her or his faith journey.

- How does your view of faith affect the way you work with children?
- How does your experience of faith affect the way you work with children?

There are a number of theories on faith development, which can underpin work with children and give a deeper understanding of the process that both children and adults go through in developing their faith. Faith isn't a package to be given to children: it is a process, through which we accompany them.

John Westerhoff, an Episcopal priest, was Professor of Theology and Christian Nurture at the Duke University Divinity School, and is a distinguished lecturer, scholar and writer. He developed a theory with a progression through four "styles of faith," outlined below.

- How do these ideas relate to your own experience of your growth of faith and the faith development of others?
- What are the implications for your work with children?

Westerhoff's Faith Development Theory

- **Experienced faith:** Theological words and doctrines are unimportant. Experiences of trust, love and acceptance provide opportunities for faith to form.
- **Affiliative faith:** Stories, experiences of awe and mystery, feelings and religious experiences combine to give a sense of belonging. There is a strong need to belong, to participate and to identify with the community of faith.
- **Searching faith:** This is a time of questioning, doubting, experimenting with other ideas and finding alternative suggestions and explanations.
- **Owned faith or mature faith:** This is a combination of the affiliative and searching

styles of faith. People now want to put their faith into personal and social action, to stand up for what they believe. Owned faith is enriched and developed by the challenge of different perspectives on the truth.

Alister Hardy, a British zoologist, believed that we are "religious animals" by nature. In surveys and research in the United Kingdom, a high proportion of adults say that they have had a spiritual experience at some time in their lives, but few of them have ever talked about it and few are involved in a formal religious institution such as a Christian church.

Read the poem, "A World Prayer," written by a nine-year-old in a school religious education lesson.

- Is there anything in the poem that surprises you?
- If we are born naturally religious, why are there not more people of all ages in the churches?

A World Prayer: Hallowed be thy name

Two tall towers,
Like two people hugging,
Praying,
"Hallowed be thy name."

A meadow of poppies,
Like a river of blood cutting through the world,
Bleeding,
"Hallowed be thy name."

A football crowd,
A symbol of sport,
Echoing,
"Hallowed be thy name."

The sticky spring water,
Trickling down the face of a thirsty child,
Laughing,
"Hallowed be thy name."

A white and black cloud,
A sign of friendship,
Touching,
"Hallowed be thy name."
© Christian Education

David Hay, a British academic, in his book, *Children and God*, says that all children are interested in four fundamental questions:

- Who am I?
- Where have I come from?
- Where am I going?
- What am I meant to do?

In order to accompany children on their journey of faith, it is necessary to allow them to explore and articulate their questions. Children need a safe space to explore these questions. As in physical and mental development, it is vital to be aware that children of the same age may not have developed to the same stage or style of faith.

- Do you agree that your role is to "accompany children on their journey of faith"? Why/why not?
- How do you encourage children to ask fundamental questions?
- How can you enable your children to grow and develop as people of faith?
- How can the church avoid making children feel that they should adopt adult religious language and activities rather than expressing their faith in their own ways?
- Think about the experiences of worship on offer to the children in your group. Are there any changes you would like to see made in the light of this session?

There are more opportunities to think about faith and spirituality in Session 6.

Biblical Thought

Jesus and Children

Read Mark 9:33-37 and 10:13-16. (Note that in Mark 9:36, the Good News Bible differs from other translations in saying that Jesus placed the child at the front.) What do these passages have to say to us about children's place and the way Jesus saw children?

Jesus placed the child at the center, where they were part of what was happening—not in front where they would be uncomfortable, not at the back where they would be uninvolved, but in the middle. What steps can you take to prevent the children in your church from feeling either uncomfortable and embarrassed or uninvolved?

There is also an implication that children have a ministry. Share your own experiences of children ministering to others. How can you make it easier for the children in your church to discover and exercise their ministries?

What do you think Jesus meant when he told his disciples to "receive the kingdom of God like a little child"?

Reflection on Learning

- What questions do you have about life and faith? Where do you look for answers?
- What do you think a new child would like or need to know about your children's group? Talk to the children in your group about this. What practical things can be done to enable a new child to settle in and want to keep being involved?

Worship

You will need:

✔ Photographs of children (cut from newspapers and magazines) showing different ages/races/abilities, different contexts, different emotions and so on

✔ A table on which to spread out the pictures, so that everyone can move around to see them

Choose one picture that "speaks" to you. What is this child's life like? What might you want to say to that child? What is that child saying to you?

Read Mark 9:33-37 and 10:13-16 again, and spend a few moments in silent reflection. Imagine the scene, including the child in the photograph. Bring that child to Jesus in your imagination. Now bring the children in your group to Jesus. What does Jesus say to them? What do they say to him? Where are you in the scene? Do you want to say anything to Jesus? What does he say to you?

Pray (aloud or silently) for the children in your group and for one another.

Suggested Songs

Father, I place into your hands (Songs of Fellowship, Kingsway)

Moses, I know you're the man (Partners in Praise, Stainer and Bell)

One more step along the world I go (Partners in Praise, Stainer and Bell)

Take, O take me as I am (Come All You People, Wild Goose Publications)

Alternatively, choose a song likely to be known by the whole group, or listen to a piece of music.

Physical Development

0 – 3 years	3 – 5 years	5 – 7 years	7 – 11 years	11 – 13 years	13+ years
Grows very quickly					
Grasps, sits					
Crawls, stands					
Walks					
Hand-eye coordination improves →→→→→→→→→→					
Talks more and more clearly					
Runs, jumps, skips →→→→→→					
Climbs, throws, catches					
Childhood illnesses →→→→→→→→→→					
		Significant improvement in physical coordination			
		Permanent teeth			
		Interest in games and other physical activities			
		Physical growth slower			
		Finer coordination			
		Restless and energetic			
			Rapid spurt of growth, especially in height		
			Conscious of physical appearance		
			Girls enter puberty →→→→→		
			Boys enter puberty →→→→→→		
				Muscular growth	
				Skin problems for many	
					Strength and coordination increase rapidly

Reproduced with permission from *Equipped to Lead* published by Discipleship Resources © 2008

Social Development

0 – 3 years	3 – 5 years	5 – 7 years	7 – 11 years	11 – 13 years	13+ years
Self-centered, dependent on parent figure(s)					
Growing bonds with family					
Often shy with strangers					
Plays alongside other children rather than with them					
	Begins to relate to adults outside family group				
	Does things with other children				
	Respects teachers and leaders; sees "big" people as good →→→→→→→				
		Eager to be accepted by others of same age →→→→→→→→→→→→→→→			
			Enjoys belonging to an organized group		
			Identifies with activity leaders, film stars, music stars, sports stars		
			Intimate affection for friend(s) of same sex		
				Forms and joins gangs, cliques	
				Growing ability to put self in others' shoes	
				May develop strong loyalty to team, teammates, school	
				Admires significant adult leaders	
				Explores relationships with opposite sex	
				Grows more distant from parents	
					Often conflict at home
					Tries out leadership skills

Mental Development

0 – 3 years	3 – 5 years	5 – 7 years	7 – 11 years	11 – 13 years	13+ years
Begins to distinguish self from other people and objects					
Imitates					
Makes things happen					
Recalls, invents					
	Asks questions, begins to converse				
		Learns best from concrete activities and objects →→→→→→			
	Confuses real and imaginary →→→				
		Forms and uses mental symbols and images			
		Classifies, relates, orders			
		Learns facts readily			
		Adds, subtracts, reads			
			Reasons logically, with concrete objects present		
			Fantasy becomes less important		
			Wants proof		
				Begins to think abstractly without using concrete objects	
				Builds concepts out of facts →→	
				Relates concepts to one another	
					Uses varied thought processes
					Develops hypotheses; considers and tests all possibilities

Moral Development

0 – 3 years	3 – 5 years	5 – 7 years	7 – 11 years	11 – 13 years	13+ years
Anything pleasant or exciting is good					
No sense of right or wrong					
Wants to please parents →→→→→→→→→					
Obeys "big" people to avoid being punished or hurt					
Obeys rules in order to receive rewards and have favors returned					
		Acts so as to please others, be liked →→→			
		Fairness is important →→→→→→→→→→→→→→→→→			
			Wants to avoid blame and guilt		
			Tries to obey the fixed social and religious rules		
				Behavior is modeled on friends and heroes/heroines	
				Begins to rebel against authority	
				Wants to do his/her duty	
					Concerned about rules and laws, either obeying or changing them

Religious Development

	0 – 3 years	3 – 5 years	5 – 7 years	7 – 11 years	11 – 13 years	13+ years
Begins to trust others, self and the environment	✓					
Learns to say "No!"	✓					
Experiences awe and wonder		✓				
Loves pattern, repetition and routine		✓				
Senses the love of parents and the Christian community →→→→→		✓				
Imitates adult religion →→→→→→→→		✓				
Asks "Why?"		✓				
Has a vivid imagination		✓				
Takes initiative; steps out alone			✓			
Begins to ask religious questions →→→→			✓			
Takes stories and symbols literally →→→→→→			✓			
Confuses fact and fiction			✓			
Believes what adults say			✓			
Responds to story-hero figures			✓			
Often finds joy and self-esteem in work and learning →→→→→→				✓		
Takes concepts as concrete: God is like a person				✓		
Begins to sort out fact from fiction				✓		
Self-esteem is important but may be shaky →→→				✓		
Develops a clearer personal identity, a sense of "who I am" and "what I stand for"					✓	
May experience a vivid sense of relationship with God					✓	
Needs to explore questions about faith and life					✓	
May make some commitment to the church						✓

Reproduced with permission from *Equipped to Lead* published by Discipleship Resources © 2008

Images of Faith

Reproduced with permission from *Equipped to Lead* published by Discipleship Resources © 2008

Personal Reflection Sheet

What did you learn from this session?

How will this affect the way you work with children?

What further items in this area would you like to follow up?

Portfolio Checklist

Learning Outcomes

- To understand how children develop physically, emotionally, intellectually, socially, morally and spiritually.

- To appreciate the range of learning styles and approaches that there can be within a group.

- To reflect on personal experience of life and faith, and the effects of this on ways of working with children.

- To consider work with children in the light of some theories of human development.

To show that the learning outcomes have been achieved, your portfolio must include at least the following. (Check when you have included each one in the file.)

☐ Personal reflection sheet

☐ Notes taken during Session 1, with any additional ideas

☐ Your paper cup and notes of what you learned through doing it

☐ "Images of faith" sheet and your reflections on it

☐ The picture you chose in worship and a note of the reason why

☐ Any other responses/reflections you wish to include

The participant's involvement in a group for Session 1, "Child Development," is confirmed. The learning outcomes have been achieved through the evidence provided.

Signed (assessor) _____ Date _____

Any comments from assessor

Signed (candidate) _____ Date _____

SESSION TWO
Leadership Skills

Aim

To enable participants to identify and reflect on their current skills and encourage them to actively seek support for themselves in their work with children.

Learning Outcomes

- To evaluate current skills, gifts, strengths and weaknesses and identify possibilities for personal development.
- To recognize the need to feel valued, equipped and supported in their role.
- To develop the skills and habit of reflecting on their work with children.

Materials Needed

Starters

- ✔ A selection of everyday objects
- ✔ Photographs of world leaders
- ✔ A flipchart, plus newspaper and sticky tape (for "Teamwork: Tower"), or construction materials and preprepared model (for "Teamwork: Model Maker")

Core

- ✔ Large sheets of paper and pens
- ✔ Pre-printed slips of paper (for Exercise C)
- ✔ "Elmer" story by David McKee (optional)

Worship

✔ Pens and plain postcards or small pieces of paper
✔ Photographs of participants, glue sticks, and laminate pouches
✔ CD and CD player

I heard the Lord ask, "Is there anyone I can send? Will someone go for us?" "I'll go," I answered. "Send me!" (Isaiah 6:8, CEV)

Starters

Everyday Objects

> **You will need:**
> ✔ A selection of everyday objects

Look at a selection of everyday objects: for example, a packet of seeds, a map, a can of beans and so on. Use these objects to make comments about leadership: for example, "Being a leader is like/is not like (a packet of seeds, a map, a can of beans and so on), because . . ."

Leaders

> **You will need:**
> ✔ Photographs of world leaders

If a set of photographs of current and past world leaders is available, look at them and discuss what are or were their strengths and weaknesses. Discuss what kind of leader is attractive and why.

Alternatively, share past memories of leaders. "I admired one leader I remember because . . ." "I disliked one leader I remember because . . ." Attempt to work out what was important to those leaders.

Teamwork

> **You will need:**
> ✔ A flipchart
> ✔ Newspaper and sticky tape (for "Tower")
> ✔ Construction materials and preprepared model (for "Model Maker")

Do *one* of the following activities.

Tower

> **You will need:**
> ✔ Newspaper and 1m sticky tape per group

In groups of four, use the newspaper and sticky tape to build the tallest tower possible in the time given.

Human Knot

In groups of four or five, form a circle, shoulder-to-shoulder. Stretch your arms out in front toward the middle of the circle and join hands with two different people. Wait, holding hands, until everyone is joined. The task for each group now is to untangle and form a new circle without anyone letting go of the hands they are holding. Participants may change their grip so as to be more comfortable, but they are not to unclasp and reclasp so as to undo the knot.

Welded Ankle

Mark off beginning and finish lines for a space across which the group must travel. The group assembles behind the start, with their feet touching a neighbor's foot on each side to form an unbroken line. They must travel across the space and over the finish line while maintaining continuous contact with their neighbors' feet. If anyone in the group loses contact, the entire group must return to the start.

Model Maker

> **You will need:**
> ✔ Bags of construction materials
> ✔ One prepared model

The leader prepares a fairly simple (but not too simple!) model using Lego, K'nex or similar, probably using 20–25 pieces. The participants are given one minute to look at the model before it is taken out of sight.

Each group is given a bag of the exact pieces needed to make an identical model, and must, working together, build an exact replica of the original model (even down to which colored bricks go where).

A time limit may be set within which the task must be completed to help focus the group (and, incidentally, adding a sense of urgency).

Teamwork Debrief and Conclusion

Whichever teamwork activity you chose to do, hold a debriefing session, asking the following questions.

- ⚙ Who took the lead?
- ⚙ What other roles were identifiable?
- ⚙ Was everyone made to feel part of the activity?
- ⚙ How was the contribution of each person valued?
- ⚙ What words or actions assisted the group?

An alternative means of debriefing is a group sculpture. Once the activity is finished, a volunteer arranges the group in a way that visually represents how the people related or worked together. This might be an abstract form or a re-creation of a still scene from the activity. Allow each person in the group in turn to step out of the sculpture and view it from different angles. The tutor could step in to take the place of each participant in turn as that person steps out. Allow the participants to comment on the sculpture and suggest how they might change it from their viewpoint, or perhaps how it might change if the group could improve on their performance.

Finally, on a sheet of flipchart paper, draw two columns, one headed "positive" and one headed "negative." List the positive aspects of working as a member of a team, and then the negative aspects.

What's in a Team? _____

> You will need:
> ✔ Large sheets of paper and pens
> ✔ Pre-printed slips of paper (for Exercise C)

Select from Exercise A, B, or C. If you are doing this session with a group of colleagues who work together, relate the questions to your specific situation, but otherwise treat them more generally.

Exercise A

Have a group wordstorm on "Ten things you could do to build a team" (being realistic about time commitments and rotas).

Exercise B

Discuss the following statements. If a team is to be effective:

- ⚙ Team members must be clear about the aim of the group.
- ⚙ Team members must have clear roles.
- ⚙ There must be effective leadership.
- ⚙ Team members must feel that their input is valued.
- ⚙ Team members should trust one another.

Can you recognize ways in which these things do or could happen in a team situation? What could be added?

Exercise C

What needs to happen in a team? Arrange the following phrases according to their importance in a children's ministry team. Add two or three if you think something is missing.

Agree on the most important one, then the next most important two, then the next most important three, and so on, to create a pyramid of important elements. Discard one or two if you can all agree.

It will be easier if you have each element printed on a separate piece of paper so that you can lay them out in priority order on the floor (see page 50 for a photocopiable list).

⚙ Develop shared aims
⚙ Ensure everyone has a clear role
⚙ Have an overall leader
⚙ Have someone to represent the team at church meetings
⚙ Make everyone feel valued
⚙ Arrange social events
⚙ Celebrate successes
⚙ Give one another feedback
⚙ Appreciate one another
⚙ Arrange regular planning meetings
⚙ Work in pairs
⚙ Pray together
⚙ Attend training regularly
⚙ Develop skills
⚙ Bring new workers to join the team
⚙ Have a Christmas party
⚙ Set a realistic budget
⚙ Get support from the whole church
⚙ [Add your own suggestions]

Support Web

You will need:
✔ "Elmer" story by David McKee (optional)

Individuals and teams need support. In a football game, there are only eleven players on the field for each team at any one time, but there is a huge support network that goes into trying to ensure that the team is as effective as possible: coach, trainer, physiotherapist, scout, doctor, substitutes, fans, and so on. On an airplane flight, you only see the pilot and the cabin crew, but there are dozens of people who designed and built the aircraft, keep it maintained, prepare meals, put the steps or ramp in place for you to get on and off, run air traffic control, and so on.

Think together about the support you are given as a team of children's workers and as individuals—and, more important, what sort of support it is. For example, the church's support may be financial support in the form of a resources budget. The support of partners or family may be in taking on additional tasks or giving permission in some way.

Individually, create a support web on a sheet of paper. This is not to be shared with anyone, but will be used later in worship.

These supporters are as much a part of the team as those who actually do the work, yet sometimes their involvement is not recognized.

You may like to read one of the "Elmer" stories by David McKee (published by Red Fox). The first story, "Elmer," is suitable. Invite the group to respond to the story.

Who's in a Team?

Dr. Meredith Belbin, a management consultant, has done some important research into team roles and effective leadership. His work with a large number of managers suggests that there are nine possible team roles that a person can adopt. Some are natural roles, some are roles that a person can adopt if necessary, and some are roles that a person finds very hard to adopt.

Study the roles in the grid on page 50. Which do you think you represent? Which roles might have been displayed in the earlier part of the session? Which roles are missing in the team you work with?

Reflection in Action

Look at the "reflection" circle below. Think together about traveling to this session. Did it involve a car? Public transportation? Walking? Sharing a ride with someone else? Were there any hold-ups? Anything unexpected? How was the timing—too early or on time? Might you do the preparation or the journey differently next time? Use a different route? Leave earlier?

We reflect on so many things during our "normal" day that it is second nature: we make decisions about the future based upon our reflections on past experiences. But we often don't use this same method in thinking about our work with children. Think back to the last session in which you were involved with children. You have already done the "Plan" and the "Do": you now need to "Reflect" and, as a result of your reflection, decide what you would do differently next time.

Individually, write down each thing you "Did" in that session, "Reflect" on it and note your reflections, even if the decision is to do the same next time. Share together any thoughts that come out of doing this exercise.

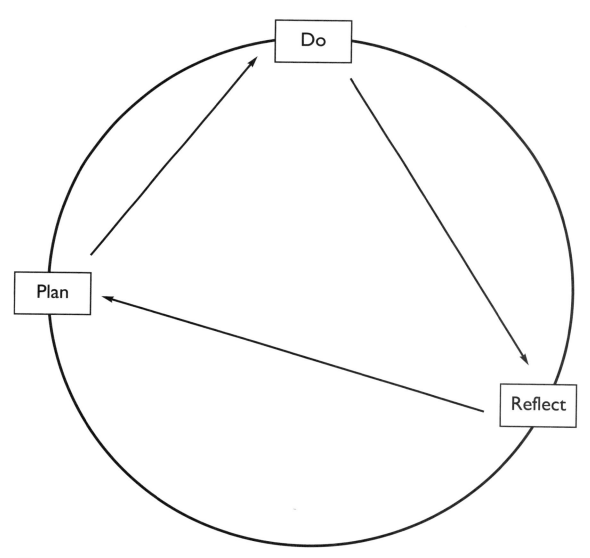

Biblical Thought

At times, we can all feel inadequate for the task ahead, but God knows each of us and calls us to work in children's ministry.

Read Psalm 139:1-6 and write down the things about you that God can use in children's ministry, both the obviously good skills, talents and experiences and the less obvious things that God is transforming and using. Share your thoughts with the group if you wish.

Then read Isaiah 42:1-4. Isaiah's prophecy highlights some qualities of the Lord's Servant, which may be important for your ministry.

- What helps you to know you are chosen and loved by God?
- What helps you to present God's love well without "shouting or raising your voice"?
- Is bringing justice for children part of your ministry?

Read any of the following passages and reflect on what they show of Jesus' leadership styles.

John 2:12-22
John 13:3-6
Luke 2:41-52
Luke 9:1-6
Luke 24:13-35
Mark 6:45-46

When might we choose certain leadership styles, and why?

What makes a good leader? Here are four key qualities:

- Leaders have vision.
- Leaders attract followers.
- Leaders can communicate their vision.
- Leaders enable the group to achieve a common goal.

This fourth quality requires many skills and attributes. Make a list together of some that Jesus seemed to possess, and share with one another some Gospel passages that might show some of Jesus' skills of leadership and teamwork.

You might like to choose from many other passages that show how Jesus exercised a variety of leadership qualities, and discuss what we can learn from these passages for our own practice. In what situations might certain styles be more effective?

Reflection on Learning

Job Advertisement

Write a job ad for the team of people you need for the children's work at your church.

Personal Development Plan

Write an individual personal development plan, detailing what you hope to be doing over the next six to twelve months. Include skills, events, experiences, training and ideas to think about—anything that will contribute to your development as a person who works with children or as a person who follows the Christian way.

Pair up with another member of the group, preferably someone from another church. Give each other a copy of your development plan and talk them through for five minutes each. Check with your "buddy" regularly, every month or every quarter (this could be a telephone call, a meeting or a social visit). The conversations should include Question 1 and at least two of the following questions:

Question 1 What has gone well since we last met?

Question 2 Have you done anything new since we last talked?

Question 3 Is there anything that hasn't gone well over the last few months?

Question 4 Is there anything that, on reflection, you would have done differently?

Question 5 What is your next "big" plan?

With others, write a possible development plan for the children's ministry team at your church. Check whether anything has previously been written and what the whole church has said about children. Include steps for individuals and the team. Consider how the children will be involved in the plan. How will thinking be shared with those not present but part of the local group?

Worship

> You will need:
> ✔ Pens and plain postcards or small pieces of paper
> ✔ Photographs of participants, glue sticks and laminate pouches
> ✔ CD and CD player

Picture the people who give you support, using the "support web" drawn earlier (see pp. 45). Recall the tower building or other team activity, and picture the people who are in your children's work team.

A Prayer

For these people, their support, their skills, their friendship and their faith, we give you thanks, Lord.

Suggested Song

"Brother, Sister, Let Me Serve You" (Sing Glory, Kevin Mayhew)

Group Affirmation Exercise

Sit in a circle and all take a small piece of paper or plain postcard. Write your name on one side of the paper and place it, facedown, in the center of the circle. Now pick up someone else's paper and write a positive appreciation on the reverse. Repeat with other papers if appropriate. Write, "We thank God for . . . in the group . . .," filling in the blank space with a positive comment about the person named.

Finally, working around the group, each read out the affirmation written on the card (but not the name). This will affirm the group for the skills that are contained within it, even though people will not know which comments relate to whom.

Music

"Together We Are Strong" (Track 1, *Small World, Big Band Volume 2—More Friends*, Jools Holland and friends)

Reading

Read this extract from a book by Albert Schweitzer.

He comes to us as one unknown, without a name, as of old, by the lakeside, he came to those men who knew him not. He speaks to us the same word: "Follow thou me!" and sets us the task, which he has to fulfil for our time. He commands. And to those who obey him, whether they be wise or simple, he will reveal himself in the toils, the conflicts, the sufferings which they shall pass through in his fellowship, and as an ineffable mystery, they shall learn in their own experience who he is.

Albert Schweitzer, The Spiritual Life (The Ecco Press, 1996)

Sending Out

Using the template below, invite participants to attach their photograph to the box, or photocopy and laminate the card using self-laminating name badge pouches (available from larger stationery stores).

Form into a "group sculpture" in preparation for blessing one another with the words of the Grace.

Finally, as a team, prepare and share coffee and cookies.

What we are is God's
gift to us.

Who we become is our
gift to God.

Eleanor Powell

What's in a Team? Exercise C

Photocopy and cut out these phrases if you wish to arrange them in priority order on the floor.

- Develop shared aims
- Ensure everyone has a clear role
- Have an overall leader
- Have someone to represent the team at church meetings
- Make everyone feel valued
- Arrange social events
- Celebrate successes
- Give one another feedback
- Appreciate one another
- Arrange regular planning meetings
- Work in pairs
- Pray together
- Attend training regularly
- Develop skills
- Bring new workers to join the team
- Have a Christmas party
- Set a realistic budget
- Get support from the whole church
- [Add your own suggestions]

Who's in a Team? Belbin's Team Roles

Plant:	very creative, the ideas person. The person who often has a game or activity to suggest for each week's theme.
Resource Investigator:	extrovert, good at making outside contacts and developing ideas. A leader able to bring new people into the children's groups, involve helpers and suggest someone or something to add to what is planned.
Monitor Evaluator:	shrewd and prudent, analytical. A children's worker who takes a broader look at what the children's group is achieving, making suggestions for the medium term, having ideas for longer-term development.
Shaper:	dynamic and challenging. The children's worker with new ideas and different ways of doing things, seeing chances to change the church's patterns.
Coordinator:	respected, mature and good at ensuring that talents are used effectively. A good leader of the children's ministry, drawing people in and playing to their strengths.
Implementer:	practical, loyal and task oriented. The group leader who can always be relied on to be there and be dependable in seeing to the practical necessities for the children and the leaders.
Completer	Finisher: meticulous and with attention to detail, also full of nervous energy. The children's worker who makes sure everything has been thought of and is well organized.
Team Worker:	caring and very people oriented. The person on the children's team who looks out for everyone on the team, checking that they are happy and supported.
Specialist:	high technical skill, and professional as opposed to organizational prime loyalties. Could be the artistic one or the person who can get children involved with the computer or the music—they love that special interest.

Reproduced with permission from *Equipped to Lead* published by Discipleship Resources © 2008

Session 2: Leadership Skills

Personal Reflection Sheet

What did you learn from this session?

[ ]

How will this affect the way you work with children?

[ ]

What further items in this area would you like to follow up?

[ ]

Reproduced with permission from *Equipped to Lead* published by Discipleship Resources © 2008

Portfolio Checklist

Learning outcomes

⚙ To evaluate current skills, gifts, strengths and weaknesses, and identify possibilities for personal development.

⚙ To recognize the need to feel valued, equipped and supported in their role.

⚙ To develop the skills and habit of reflecting on their work with children.

To show that the learning outcomes have been achieved, your portfolio must include at least the following. (Check when you have included each one in the file.)

☐ Personal reflection sheet

☐ Notes taken during Session 2, with any additional ideas

☐ Your comments and ideas about being part of a team

☐ Your reflection exercise on a session with children

☐ Your support web and any affirming items from worship

☐ Your personal development plan (use the method suggested or another)

☐ Any other responses/reflections you wish to include

The participant's involvement in a group for Session 2, "Leadership skills," is confirmed. The learning outcomes have been achieved through the evidence provided.

Signed (assessor) _____Date _____

Any comments from assessor

Signed (candidate) _____Date _____

SESSION THREE
Program Planning

Aim

To develop an understanding of how children learn and the skills required to deliver a program relevant to their needs.

Learning Outcomes

- To understand how learning styles in childhood differ, and are influenced by society and culture.
- To work creatively with children, using a variety of learning styles.
- To plan original sessions and deliver published programs to meet the needs of children.
- To develop the practice of reflecting on and evaluating sessions.

Materials Needed

Starters
✔ An apple
✔ French objects

Core
✔ Flipchart
✔ An example of an online learning style questionnaire

- ✔ *Alfie Gives a Hand* by Shirley Hughes (published by Red Fox) or similar story
- ✔ Resources for children's groups that have been found useful
- ✔ A range of current worship and learning materials
- ✔ Paper and pens
- ✔ Post-it® notes
- ✔ Candy bar

Worship

- ✔ CD and CD player
- ✔ A table-size cross and clay or play dough

Opening Thought

They said to Jesus, "We need more confidence!" Jesus said, "A bit of trust is all you need, the sort a gardener has. If you have a small seed you can make it grow into a large plant. Or you can transplant a bush from a garden to a new position by the sea and it will thrive." (Luke 17:5–6, from John Henson, *Good as New*, O Books, 2004)

Starters

Apple

> **You will need:**
> ✔ An apple

Set an apple in the center of the group. How could it be used? Call out as many uses as possible in two minutes. Ask each person, if she or he had to choose only one use, what would it be and why? Then ask each person to think of a child he or she knows. What might that child choose?

France

This activity can be based on a different country of the world, if that would be easier to prepare.

> **You will need:**
> ✔ French objects

Pass around:

- A baguette and a round of camembert. Invite everyone to break off bits to eat as the other items are passed round.
- A euro.
- A souvenir from France.
- A travel brochure for France.
- A picture from a French gallery.
- A guidebook held open with rubber bands at a page of text with a picture of a French city.
- A library book on the history of France, open at a page of text.

When all the items have been circulated, tell of an experience in France.

Core

Learning Styles

> **You will need:**
> ✔ Flipchart
> ✔ *Alfie Gives a Hand* by Shirley Hughes, or similar story

A number of theories have been developed about the different ways in which people learn, and which styles an individual might find most helpful. There is no "best style" that fits everyone or that everyone needs to use; they all have advantages. It is useful if those preparing sessions are aware of their own learning preference, because there can be a tendency to use the preferred style most often. Deliberately varying the learning style being used in a group enriches the experience for everyone.

What can you recall from the exercise about France? Do members of the group differ in what they remember first? Why?

The following are some labels given to learning styles in a model called VARK.

Which do you think best describes you?

- **Visual:** Learn best by seeing (pictures, diagrams, multimedia and so on). Enjoy finding a new place by using a map.
- **Aural:** Learn best by hearing (a discussion, a speaker who tells stories to illustrate a point and so on). Enjoy debate and exploring ideas out loud.
- **Read/Write:** Learn best by reading (a leaflet, handout, written information and so on). Enjoy looking up information in text.
- **Kinesthetic:** Learn best through action (trying things out, doing activities along-

side someone else, and so on). Enjoy getting out and doing things.

Clearly no one learns in only one style, but most people have a clear preference. A variety of styles can be helpful to individuals and is a must to include everyone in a group.

There are fun questionnaires online to find out more about your learning style. VARK is only one example; typing "learning styles" into an Internet search engine will turn up a multitude of possibilities.

On the flipchart, list different methods that could be used to explore the parable of the lost sheep (Luke 15:1–7) with a group of children that includes all the above learning styles.

Discuss ways in which a children's picture book, such as *Alfie Gives a Hand* by Shirley Hughes, can be used:

⚙ To make a point about sharing.

⚙ As a stimulus for making a model.

⚙ As the beginning of a discussion about hunting for something lost.

⚙ For remembering experiences together.

⚙ For talking about the way we try something to find out how it works.

Planning a Session

NAOMIE

The acronym NAOMIE is a mnemonic to aid preparation.

⚙ **Need:** What do the children need? What do we, the leaders (and any other interested adults), need?

⚙ **Aim:** What should be achieved by the end of the session?

⚙ **Objectives:** What are the smaller goals that work together to achieve the aim?

⚙ **Method:** What methods will be used? What talents are there to be used? Are they varied? Are they suitable for use with dif-

ferent children? Is there a balance of active and reflective methods? Is the program inclusive?

⚙ **Implementation:** Does everyone know his or her responsibilities? Is everyone able to do what is required of him or her?

⚙ **Evaluation:** How did it go? What went well? Why? Did the session fulfill the aim? What could have been better? How? What needs to be remembered next time? (Anecdotes can contribute to evaluation.)

Selecting Published Material

You will need:

✔ Resources for children's groups that have been found useful

What matters when choosing which material to use? Rate the following statements from 1 to 5, with 1 being "very important" and 5 "not important at all."

1. The resource offers a stand-alone selection of material for each week throughout the year
   1 2 3 4 5

2. It follows the Revised Common Lectionary
   1 2 3 4 5

3. It highlights all the festivals of the Christian year
   1 2 3 4 5

4. It gives plenty of choices for a wide range of ages of children in the one magazine
   1 2 3 4 5

5. It uses inclusive language
   1 2 3 4 5

6. It has plenty of ideas of things to make and do
   1 2 3 4 5

7. Material written for use with children links with companion material for a whole congregation
   1 2 3 4 5

8. Suggestions are given for worship when all ages are together
1 2 3 4 5

9. It is inexpensive
1 2 3 4 5

10. It is brightly colored
1 2 3 4 5

11. It can be picked up and used easily
1 2 3 4 5

12. Someone trustworthy recommended it
1 2 3 4 5

13. The local church has always used it
1 2 3 4 5

14. It is photocopiable
1 2 3 4 5

15. It is firmly biblically based
1 2 3 4 5

16. It has a spiritual element
1 2 3 4 5

17. It contains plenty of web links and resources on the website
1 2 3 4 5

18. Everything comes in the pack
1 2 3 4 5

19. Activity papers are included
1 2 3 4 5

Examine a selection of materials and see which product(s) most closely fulfill(s) the needs identified.

Using Published Material

The following pointers could be answered with a quick "yes/no." However, you may want to respond "Maybe, if . . ."

⚙ Should every leader have his or her own copy of the material?

⚙ Would you write on your copy?

⚙ Should material be selected bearing in mind learning styles—of both leaders and children?

⚙ Should the leaders meet to prepare? How often?

⚙ Might material be prepared that is not used?

Finally, think about what simple ways can be adopted to ensure that everyone knows who is doing or bringing what for a session. How can people let others know if they can't attend?

Devising New Themes

What might cause a decision not to use a specific week of published material? Is there a clear need to be addressed, which would require an alternative program? Choose a scenario such as the sudden death of a much-loved member of the community, a national disaster, or a specific event in the life of the church, and use your usual program pattern as the basis for a suitable session.

Practice

You will need:
✔ Resources for children's groups that have been found useful
✔ A range of current worship and learning materials

Divide into two groups to plan a session for a specific group of children (real or imagined). Ask one group to use a published program (either one they are used to, or an unfamiliar one) as the basis for the session. Ask the other group to use material from a variety of sources, selecting from those provided and choosing a theme relevant to their community.

Look at and briefly discuss the NAOMIE method of planning (see above) before starting. Afterward, share the resulting session plans and discuss how they might work. If possible, use the plans to run a real session, and meet together afterward to discuss how well they worked. Comment on the work of the other group.

Devise a way of reflecting on a session as soon as it finishes, based on the "Evaluation" part of NAOMIE (see page 62).

Evaluating Other Resources

Spend ten minutes discussing the following questions.

- Where can resources be found?
- What resources have others found useful, and why?
- What works well for leaders and for children?
- How is that evaluation made?
- What are the key things to look for in a resource?

Question

> You will need:
> ✔ Paper and pens

Asking questions is often used as a method in children's groups, but there are many sorts of questions and different reasons for asking them. Make a list of reasons for asking questions.

Some questions are "open": for example, "What might it feel like to be lost?" Some are "closed": for example, "How many sheep were lost?" Different types of question are appropriate or inappropriate in different circumstances.

Thinking about the Bible story of Jesus' baptism (Matthew 3:13–17), look at the questions below. Which might be used or not, and why?

- Who was there? What was the name of the river?
- What did John say? What did Jesus say? What did God say?

- What sounds would the people watching hear?
- What might the people be thinking?
- What would you ask if you were there?

Further discussion or reflection on the topic of questions should include:

- What are the pros and cons of beginning a session with the question "Who can remember what we did last week?"
- What types of question should be avoided?
- What are helpful responses to answers given to questions?

Play

> You will need:
> ✔ Post-it® notes
> ✔ Flipchart
> ✔ Candy bar

Play is a vital way of learning for children. Individually, bring to mind a favorite play activity from your childhood. Draw or briefly describe it on a Post-it® note, and stick the note on the flipchart. Now, on that flipchart sheet, add a list of the opportunities for play that exist in the life of your church today.

Share a candy bar and discuss whether "work, rest, and play" are really three different things.

Discuss the following quotation: "The main characteristic of play—child or adult—is not its content, but its mode. Play is an approach to action, not a form of activity" (Jerome Bruner, quoted in Janet Moyles, *Just Playing?*, OUP, 1989).

When might play feature in a session—at the beginning, in the middle, or at the end?

What are the advantages of each? Think of some examples.

Biblical Thought

Jesus used different teaching styles, which met the differing preferences of his hearers and disciples. Some examples are:

- The good Samaritan (aural): Luke 10:30–37
- A tree and its fruit (visual): Matthew 12:33
- The feeding of the five thousand (kinesthetic): Matthew 14:13–21; Mark 6:30–44; Luke 9:10–17; John 6:1–14

There is a lack of reference in the Bible to reading and writing, as most people in Jesus' time did not have these skills. Interestingly, most of our teaching and learning now involves reading. The passage in which Jesus reads the scriptures, in Luke 4:16–22, shows how special and different reading was.

Discuss more examples of the varieties of learning that happened when people were with Jesus. Look at his actions, his ways of talking and the types of questions he used.

Reflection on Learning

- What is it important to remember when leading a session with children? Why?
- What are good methods for involving children in evaluation, using pictures, words or conversations?
- How were questions used in this session?
- Listen for questions in a future session; make a list and reflect on their use.

Worship

You will need:
- ✔ CD and CD player
- ✔ A table, tablecloth, table-size cross, and clay or play dough

Listening to a selection of majestic, crashing, bold, brash music, use lumps of clay (or playdough) to express a response to the session. Anyone who has finished with his or her shape while others are continuing to work can be still or browse a resource.

Place the shapes around the cross on a table covered with a cloth. This can be done in turn, silently or with a comment from the maker if they wish.

Read the opening thought for this session:

They said to Jesus, "We need more confidence!" Jesus said, "A bit of trust is all you need, the sort a gardener has. If you have a small seed you can make it grow into a large plant. Or you can transplant a bush from a garden to a new position by the sea and it will thrive." (Luke 17:5–6, John Henson, *Good as New*)

Sing a simple refrain, which could involve clapping, and for which the group need no written words. For example, "I've seen the light, and that's why my heart sings" (*Junior Praise 1*, Marshall Pickering)

Personal Reflection Sheet

What did you learn from this session?

How will this affect the way you work with children?

What further items in this area would you like to follow up?

Portfolio Checklist

Learning Outcomes

⚙ To understand how learning styles in childhood differ, and are influenced by society and culture.

⚙ To work creatively with children, using a variety of learning styles.

⚙ To plan original sessions and deliver published programs to meet the needs of children.

⚙ To develop the practice of reflecting on and evaluating sessions.

To show that the learning outcomes have been achieved, your portfolio must include at least the following. (Check when you have included each one in the file.)

☐ Personal reflection sheet

☐ Notes taken during Session 3, with any additional ideas

☐ A description of your learning style

☐ The session you planned with the group

☐ An outline of a session you have used and your evaluation of it, using the method you devised

☐ The clay model (or a picture of it) that you made in worship

☐ Any other responses/reflections you wish to include

The participant's involvement in a group for Session 3, "Program Planning," is confirmed. The learning outcomes have been achieved through the evidence provided.

Signed (assessor) _____Date _____

Any comments from assessor

Signed (candidate) _____ Date _____

Reproduced with permission from *Equipped to Lead* published by Discipleship Resources © 2008

SESSION FOUR
Children and Community

Aim

To explore ways of working among children in a variety of contexts, including local, national and global.

Learning Outcomes

- To reflect on stories from different contexts and distill principles of good practice.
- To develop strategies for developing new areas of work with children in a variety of contexts.
- To explore an understanding of what it means to be "church."
- To advocate the active participation of children in mission and ministry.

Materials Needed

Starters

✔ Flipchart sheets
✔ Pens
✔ Pieces of paper of postcard size

Core

✔ Copies of stories photocopied from pages 68–70
✔ Three large sheets of paper

✔ Pens
✔ Copies of the "Planning chart" template

Worship

✔ Picture or model of a sheepfold
✔ Pieces of 8½ x 11 card stock
✔ Pencils
✔ Scissors
✔ Reflective music and CD player

Opening Thought

Children have a ministry both within and beyond the church community. They may act as evangelists among their friends or families. Many parents have been drawn to Christian commitment through their children. Children may have an apostolic ministry in being sent out to the places where children are, making Christ present in the world. Within the playground, they may work against bullying and racism, befriend the lonely or show a generosity of spirit, all of which makes the Spirit of Christ evident in other children. CGMC, *Unfinished Business* 5.12

"When you welcome one of these children because of me, you welcome me." (Matthew 18:5, CEV)

Starters

Brainstorm

> You will need:
> - ✔ Flipchart sheets
> - ✔ Pens

In small groups, brainstorm all the good things that happen in the work among children in your church community.

Church or Not Church?

> You will need:
> - ✔ Pieces of paper of postcard size
> - ✔ Pens

On separate small pieces of paper, write down the numerous different activities that children might be involved with in their community. The activities should include a wide range of things: some that are clearly "church" (for example, meeting with friends to pray), some that could be church outreach (for example, playing football), and some things that are definitely not church (for example, horse riding, life saving, judo, and so on).

When the task is complete, sort the activities into piles of "church" and "not church" according to whether the activities could be a form of church. Discuss why they belong in one pile or another. Is it the activities or the context in which they are done that makes them "church"? What is the difference between "church" and the local Christian community?

Behind the Door

Individually, think quietly about a time when you entered an unfamiliar situation—perhaps, a time when you had to go through a door not knowing who or what was behind it. Can you remember how you felt? What made you feel uncomfortable or comfortable? What did you find behind the door?

In small groups, share this experience of going into the unknown. As a whole group, talk about a scene such as the one in the film *Billy Elliott* where Billy enters the ballet class or audition room. Discuss what his feelings might have been.

What might it feel like for young people to join a minority activity, such as ballet for boys? What might it feel like for a child to cross the threshold of the church for the first time? What are the negative or positive things about the experience?

Core

Working among Children in Different Contexts

> You will need:
> - ✔ Stories photocopied from pages 68-70

For 200 years, many, if not most, children received Christian teaching and nurture in Sunday school. Today, the whole ethos of Sunday has changed. Many people regard Sunday as a day for various shopping, DIY or leisure activities, or for spending time with separated parents or grandparents. A large majority of families in today's society have no contact with the church whatsoever.

The settings in which churches work with children are now more varied than ever. Rural, urban and suburban communities often have very different needs, and the multicultural and multi-faith facets of society bring rich possibilities. Changes in the view of the place of the child in society have been mirrored by changes in the church's attitude toward children.

Read the Charter for Children and the Church from the United Reformed Church (below). Does this resemble the church you know?

1. Children are equal partners with adults in the life of the church.
2. The full diet of Christian worship is for children as well as adults.
3. Learning is for the whole church—adults and children.
4. Fellowship is for all, each belonging meaningfully to the rest.
5. Service is for children to give, as well as adults.
6. The call to evangelism comes to all God's people of whatever age.
7. The Holy Spirit speaks powerfully through children as well as adults.
8. The discovery and development of gifts in children and adults is a key function of the church.
9. As a church community, we must learn to do only those things in separate age groups that we cannot in all conscience do together.
10. The concept of the "priesthood of all believers" includes children.

Much has been written about new and different ways and styles that make it possible, in this new situation, for children and families to be in contact and involved with activities of the church community.

For all these reasons, large numbers of children participate in church activities midweek, and informal teaching is offered in a wide variety of contexts and situations. Although these events may not happen in a church building, these children are perceived as being part of the church community or simply "being church," whether they have contact with the church on Sunday or not. Such new expressions give many children and young families, who would otherwise be denied it, access to the Christian message and to safe and loving Christian communities. Many church members now see activities other than Sunday worship as "church," and groups other than the Sunday congregation as "church."

In small groups, look at two or three of the following stories.

Traveling Church

An urban church has purchased and converted a bus, which travels around local urban estates, offering monthly after-school activities and worship for children aged 7–11. The church is meeting people where they are, and children and their families are hearing about God in a relevant way. The church anticipates that, in time, sustainable Christian communities will develop in these areas.

Parents and Toddlers Praise

Parents and toddlers meet weekly in the church hall for a short fun time of praise, games and a story followed by refreshments. During refreshment time, the toddlers and parents do crafts, which provides a good opportunity for sharing fun and fellowship. The end product is something for the parents and children to take home as a reminder of the day's focus. At the end of the session, everyone either goes home or to meet older brothers or sisters from school.

Summer Club

About 50 children of primary school age live on an estate near the church in a suburban village. For the past two years, a member of the congregation has organized a summer club, with 15 children aged 8–13 attending. The aim is to reach youngsters living on the doorstep of the church. Initially, every family on the estate was visited and leaflets were delivered. The club meets twice weekly throughout the summer holidays in a variety of venues, and involves a wide range of activities (fishing, farm visits, games and so on). There is no formal Christian teaching except when discussions arise spontaneously.

The School Is Church

This is a church primary school, which holds a weekly service of Holy Communion. The children write the prayers, plan the readings and lead the music. Any child in Key Stage 2 may be prepared to receive holy communion. The whole ethos of the school is founded on prayer. Children may ask staff to be sponsors and prayer partners, and each young child is given an older child to help with problems. Children see school as a safe place where each person is valued.

Toddler Church

The new minister arrived in the small market town to find an elderly congregation and no children's work. He had two young children of his own. Through contacts made by him and his wife, toddler church now meets monthly on Saturday mornings in the children's corner of the church, for a 20-minute service in which the children participate actively. They first toll the bell and light the candles. There are three hymns (action, instrumental and traditional) and a teaching slot that involves the children in an activity. Elements of the monthly family Eucharist are included in the service, so that if families do start coming to family Eucharist, there will be some familiarity. After the service there is a time for refreshment and fellowship.

Midweek All-Age Worship

In a small market town, "Sunday" Club now meets on Thursday evenings. The children don't like church because it's boring, and the church members don't like children disturbing their traditional services. So, once a month, church members go along on a Thursday and join in the singing, watch the drama and listen to the children reading or reciting a story. It's not in church, it's not on Sunday, but it is worship.

Godly Play

This church has introduced Godly Play to its Sunday Club, with some success. Everyone sits on the floor in a circle, creating a sacred space. Behind the storyteller, there is a focal table with a nativity set, a cross, a picture of the risen Jesus, a candle and a good shepherd model. Stories are told using simple materials, many of which are three-dimensional. Open, wondering questions follow the story, and then the children respond by choosing a creative activity, which reflects what they feel about the story. This all provides a safe space, allowing children to "play with" the stories of God. Sunday Club later joins the rest of the congregation to share what has been done. The enthusiasm of the children has intrigued and excited the adult members, who are wondering what is happening.

Festival Activities

This church provided a Saturday Club in the run-up to Christmas, using the Advent season to tell the Christmas story and make decorations and presents. It culminated in a candlelit service for the children and their parents and the whole church family on Christmas Eve. This was so successful that it will be extended to a club during Lent.

Church Football Team

This church was losing all the boys from its children's group to football, baseball and so on.

It decided to change the timing of the group and recruited a football team, which included former members of the group, to take part in a local league.

Ecumenical Children's Club

Churches in several villages in the Scottish Borders had no children's work, although there were many children living in the community. They pooled their resources to provide an ecumenical midweek after-school club. On a quarterly basis, this links into the family service, which is hosted by each church in turn.

In the light of these stories, discuss:

- ⚙ What makes these activities successful?
- ⚙ What are the principles underlying them? (For example, relationships, being on the children's "turf," fun, creativity, space to just "be.")
- ⚙ What principles could you take from these clubs and apply to your own situation?
- ⚙ What things are not applicable to your situation, and why not?
- ⚙ How are these activities an expression of "church"?
- ⚙ What is already happening or could happen where you are, which is a new expression of being church?

A Strategy for New Work in Church Communities

In small groups, work through the following five steps, allowing equal time for each. Group with others from the same church or in mixed groups, where each participant thinks about his or her own community and church but shares his or her thinking with the group as they go along.

There will be insufficient time in the session to do more than begin each step and raise some of the issues. It is hoped that participants will wish to continue or take discussions further individually, together or in their church group.

Step 1: Identify the Needs of an Area

> You will need:
> ✔ Two large sheets of paper
> ✔ Pens

In the center of a large sheet of paper, draw a symbol to represent children. Around the symbol, write down the needs of the children in the community. Their needs might be physical, spiritual, emotional, mental, or social.

In the center of a second sheet, draw the same symbol and write the name of your area underneath. Write down all the different things (people, organizations and activities) in the area that relate to the children. (They may include schools, parent and toddler groups, community workers, health visitors, and leisure activities.)

If you don't know all that is available, how could you find it out?

On the second sheet, underneath the people, organizations and activities, write down what needs these things aim to meet. Think about and list the needs that remain unmet.

After this session, talk with a group of children from your church, school or community group to find out their needs and interests (taking care not to raise expectations that cannot be met).

Step 2: Acknowledge the Skills of the Church Community

> You will need:
> ✔ A large sheet of paper
> ✔ Pens

Draw a picture of a church building in the center of a large sheet of paper. Brainstorm all the different assets the church has, both physical (the building, facilities, equipment and so on) and availability of people and skills (include life skills and personality types: for example, the grandmother figure who gets alongside children, making them feel special, and the "spiritual" person who is able to offer prayerful support).

Step 3: Identify Strengths and Weaknesses of the Church Community

What is your church able to offer to the local community? Are there ways in which your church can meet the needs of the local area? A good way of assessing is to look at your church using the SWOT analysis system.

- **Strengths:** what is being done and the resources, people and buildings available.
- **Weaknesses:** what you fail to do, or do ineffectively.
- **Opportunities** in the local community. For example, the needs and opportunities that are there to reach out to children, or the opportunities to share with the congregation of your church.
- **Threats:** the potential stumbling blocks. For example, the limits of the church building, the limited number of people to do the work, people with insufficient skills and knowledge, and so on.

The church needs to be aware of current initiatives and local and national government legislation. Current laws and regulations affect the way we do things. These factors might be considered in the SWOT analysis.

Step 4: Plan Aims and Strategy

Select one or two needs of the local area, which you think need consideration. How might you start to meet these needs? How will you know

when you have met them? One planning method is the use of SMART goals. Here is the *Equipped* version.

- **Specific:** For example, an aim that says, "to be there for local children" is good but too vague. You will never know if you've met it, and then people will get discouraged. An aim "to provide regular opportunities for local children to talk about what is troubling them" is a lot clearer.
- **Measurable:** For example, "by the end of August we will have run a holiday club for one week."
- **Attributable:** Tasks should be assigned to specific people so that everyone is aware of their responsibilities.
- **Realistic:** The task should be a small step forward, not a giant leap. The aim should be attainable: for example, "the weekly after-school club should have at least five new members by Christmas" rather than "the after-school club should triple its membership by next month."
- **Timebound:** The goal should be attained within a specific timescale, giving you a clear indicator of achievement. Having a timebound goal enables you to look back and, if you've set your goals right, celebrate your success.

Step 5: Achieve the Goal

You will need:

✔ Copies of the "Planning Chart" template on page 75

A planning chart might be used to plan out the task. First the goal is set, and then the plan broken down into tasks that need to be achieved to meet that goal. At the top of the chart is a timeframe, and at the right-hand side is the list of who is responsible for each task. This shows clearly who is responsible for what, in achieving each step and checking whether the whole task is on target.

The example on page 74 indicates how this method could be used in setting up a midweek club. Select one of the SMART aims identified in Step 4. Then work out the steps that are involved in achieving it, and make a planning chart. There is a blank chart template on page 75.

Children and the Wider Community

The word "community" in the title of this session cannot be simply understood as relating to the place, village, town or suburb where the group meets. Children are part of a country and a world in which they have to learn to play their part. God's love and concern for justice are about the whole of God's people and the whole of God's world.

What can you do to bring the global community into your children's work?

⚙ Do the images that children see of Jesus show him as someone from the Middle East?

⚙ Are religious pictures on walls and in books representative of the worldwide nature of the Church?

⚙ Can children learn about the activity of the Church throughout our country and in the rest of the world?

⚙ From the learning that happens in your church, would people realize that most Christians are black?

⚙ What signs are there in your church that Christianity is a worldwide movement concerned about justice?

Look at *The Christ We Share*, a pack of pictures of Jesus from around the world (published by CMS and The Methodist Church).

Biblical Thought

In small groups, read one of the following Bible passages: Isaiah 58; Matthew 18:1-6; Matthew 25:31-46; Matthew 28:18-20.

⚙ Why should we be concerned about children in different contexts?

⚙ What might each passage have to say on this issue?

Reflection on Learning

⚙ What concerns and challenges has this session raised for you?

⚙ What potential benefits do you see for the children in your group and for your church community?

⚙ What would you like to explore further?

⚙ What action will you take or encourage your church community to take as a result of this session?

Worship

You will need:
✔ Picture or model of a sheepfold
✔ Pieces of 8½ x 11 card stock
✔ Pencils
✔ Scissors
✔ Reflective music and CD player

In the center of the room, create a sheepfold as a focus. Read John 10:7-9, about the door and the sheepfold. Draw round your foot on a piece of card stock and cut out the shape.

Think about the sheepfold as one that the children can move in and out of, to find a safe, supportive and receptive church community. Think about the steps that could be taken to ensure that this happens in your community. These thoughts can be written on the foot shape during a time of silence or appropriate peaceful music. Place the feet in front of the sheepfold.

In a time of prayer, thank God for the strengths of the church in which you worship and for opportunities to be "church" in your local community. Pray for God's help in overcoming obstacles in what you plan to do.

A Prayer

Loving Lord, open our eyes to see the need for change within our communities, give us the vision to take up these opportunities, and grant us the humility to accept those things we cannot change. Amen.

Suitable Hymns and Songs

"The Spirit lives to set us free" (*Mission Praise,* Marshall Pickering)

"Loving shepherd of thy sheep" (*Hymns for Today's Church,* Hodder & Stoughton)

"As we are gathered" (*Songs of Fellowship,* Kingsway)

"He came down that we may have love" (*Many and Great,* Wild Goose Publications)

Planning Chart for a Midweek Club

Week commencing Task	7 March	14 March	21 March	28 March	4 April	11 April	18 April	25 April	2 May	9 May	Who?
Research needs of children											All
Find out what nights current clubs meet											Leader 1
Find program materials											Leader 2
Meet to decide night and plan program											All
Contact schools to arrange to publicize club											Leader 3
Make publicity materials											Leaders 1 and 2
Prepare program											All
Publicize club in schools											Leader 3
Posters up in shops and so on											Leader 2
Meet to pray and go over final details											All
Club starts											All

Reproduced with permission from *Equipped to Lead* published by Discipleship Resources © 2008

Planning Chart Template

Week commencing											
Task	Who?										

Reproduced with permission from *Equipped to Lead* published by Discipleship Resources © 2008

Personal Reflection Sheet

What did you learn from this session?

```



```

How will this affect the way you work with children?

```



```

What further items in this area would you like to follow up?

```



```

Portfolio Checklist

Learning outcomes

⚙ To reflect on stories from different contexts and distill principles of good practice.

⚙ To develop strategies for developing new areas of work with children in a variety of contexts.

⚙ To explore an understanding of what it means to be church.

⚙ To advocate the active participation of children in mission and ministry.

To show that the learning outcomes have been achieved, your portfolio must include at least the following. (Check when you have included each one in the file.)

☐ Personal reflection sheet

☐ Notes you have taken during Session 4

☐ Your ideas in response to "The Charter for Children and the Church"

☐ Lists of the needs of your area

☐ SWOT analysis of your church

☐ The project description and planning chart

☐ The foot shape from the worship

☐ Any other answers/reflections you wish to include

The participant's involvement in a group for Session 4, "Children and Community," is confirmed. The learning outcomes have been achieved through the evidence provided.

Signed (assessor) _____Date _____

Any comments from assessor

Signed (candidate) _____ Date _____

SESSION FIVE
Pastoral Awareness

Aim

To explore the pastoral issues involved in working with children and reflect on practice.

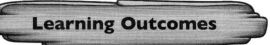
Learning Outcomes

⚙ To share insights about a variety of pastoral issues.

⚙ To explore how power is used in working with children.

⚙ To identify issues involved in providing a safe environment, physically, emotionally and spiritually, for children.

Materials Needed

Starters

✔ CD or tape player and appropriate theme tune (see below)

Core

✔ Flipchart

✔ Sheets of paper and pens

✔ "Risk Assessment Recording Table" photocopied from page 87

Biblical Thought

Photographs of children (cut from newspapers and magazines) showing different ages/races/abilities, different contexts, different emotions and/or postcards collected from art galleries, commercial sets from publishers and greetings cards

Opening Thought

God has no specific age, gender, race, physical ability or personality type as a preferred model for a human being made in the image of God (Genesis 1:26). The glorious picture of all being one in Christ with God, living in companionship, peace and joy, implies that, of course, children have a valued place in God's realm. They are to be included and cherished along with everyone else. It seems imaginable that God might say, "Children are just like me!"

Starters

Who Will It Be? _____

> You will need:
> ✔ CD or tape player and appropriate theme tune (see below)

Read aloud the following story of how not to start a training session, complete with CD player and appropriate theme tune if it is available.

This is the story of a training session carried out one evening, far away from here. The group of leaders sat close together on hard, uncomfortable chairs, in a cold room with a stale smell. In came the trainer, tall and intimidating—like an old teacher who had walked so many times into so many classrooms full of so many pupils. He placed a tape recorder on the floor and switched it on. As the tape started, he announced that he would shortly be picking someone to act out the character from the tape. Across the room came the well-known tune of a children's television program.

The participants in the group didn't know where to look. Some looked at the floor, some stared at the ceiling and some looked the trainer straight in the eye in order to take him on. As the music drew to an end, the group became more nervous: they had not come to the training session to be humiliated, but to learn. The trainer then walked around the group, ready to pounce on his victim. He picked the quietest leader, who by now was in a cold sweat . . .

Discuss the story together, including questions such as:

⚙ What might the leaders have felt when the trainer came in?

⚙ How might they have reacted to the task?
⚙ What might have happened next?

Leaders in children's groups have the power to encourage and affirm, but also to embarrass and humiliate. It is quite possible, with every good intention, to undertake activities with children, assuming that they will like them, without taking time to find out what the group's reactions are. That way, we can end up making some members of the group feel discontented or uncomfortable.

Core

Power _____

> You will need:
> ✔ Flipchart
> ✔ Sheets of paper and pens

In small groups, discuss the following questions. Record your answers on flipchart paper.

⚙ Who has the most power in the running of your children's group?
⚙ Give some examples of how leaders can use power to have a positive impact on a children's group.
⚙ Give some examples of how leaders can use power to have a negative impact on a children's group.
⚙ Read Luke 2:41–50. Who had the power in this situation? Why do you think Jesus' parents failed to see the purpose of Jesus' activity? Give examples of how we fail to allow children to express their opinions and how we devalue their role in the church.

All together, share some points from the discussions.

Misusing Power in Worship ___ 🔨

In small groups, share positive experiences of involving children in worship.

Discuss whether children are damaged, marginalized, neglected, ignored, excluded, demeaned or emotionally misused in God's realm when:

- ⚙ They are "picked on" to answer a question.
- ⚙ They are made to feel foolish because of their lack of knowledge.
- ⚙ They are used as token participants ("hold this"; "be the butt of a joke"; "accessorize me").
- ⚙ They are used to read something that someone else has written or decided is suitable.
- ⚙ They are only invited to respond to closed questions with "right" answers.
- ⚙ Their opinions and ideas are not sought.
- ⚙ They are allocated sound effect noises and gimmick involvement.
- ⚙ They are patronized.
- ⚙ Their trust is manipulated for the entertainment of others.
- ⚙ They are clapped for after a contribution, but no one else is applauded.
- ⚙ They are instructed in performing an item without consultation or explanation.
- ⚙ They are viewed as recipients of entertainment designed to keep them "being good" and "sitting still."
- ⚙ They are told the "right" interpretation of scripture as perceived by the adults.
- ⚙ Their vulnerability is exploited for the benefit of adults.
- ⚙ Their concerns are ignored in the intercessions and other parts of the worship.

Behavior _____ 🔨

Every single one of us, child and adult alike, is precious to God, made in God's image and for God's glory, made to become like Christ and be fashioned by his Spirit. Every single one of us is also vulnerable at different times and in different ways, whatever our age, experience and devotion to the Lord and to our ministry. We can all be vulnerable to temptation, tiredness, irritability, loss of self-control and unguarded words and actions.

The value that Jesus places on a child is immense, and he wants us to value children in the same way: we ignore this fact at our peril! It is not that he wants fear to be the motivation for our response to children, but he does want our hearts to beat to the same rhythm as his when it comes to loving and respecting them.

The principles embraced by churches in their child protection polices are designed to support and protect each adult and young person in the complex strengths and vulnerabilities of our relationships with one another. The principles are not intended to threaten work with children but to support it and to strengthen the sense of personal and team responsibility.

In small groups or all together, answer the following questions:

- ⚙ What words or forms of speech would you not use in front of a child, and why?
- ⚙ In what ways do we "control" children in our children's group? For example, can we run a children's group without shouting?

Share your thoughts on the following two stories about controlling children.

Story 1: *In an inner-city group in Glasgow, children were asked what was good about their particular group. Their reply was, "The leaders don't shout at you." A leader who* heard this commented, "I don't shout in my children's group. I find the use of a whistle much more effective in controlling them." Another leader said, "I think I have failed if I have to shout at the children I work with." How might this discussion continue?

Story 2: *A children's commissioner came to visit a school and asked the children if they had any questions. One child asked a question and, before the commissioner could reply, a teacher told the child off for asking a stupid question. The commissioner, irate at the teacher, replied and informed the group that the only stupid question is the one that is not asked.*

The Basics for a Positive Session with Children _____

Look at the following list of requirements for a positive session. Discuss your responses, sharing situations when you have met the children's needs in any of these ways, and adding any others to the list.

By our own behavior we offer our best and live up to our calling. Children need:

- **to know they are welcome:** They are greeted genuinely by name and they are encouraged to greet all others in the learning community.

- **to see that their place is ready:** The meeting place is comfortable and attractively prepared and there are things to do from the moment they arrive.

- **to be safe:** There are no hazards in the room and any "community rules" are known and understood by all.

- **to have your attention:** Everything is prepared, the running order is planned, and the children are the focus for the time you have together.

- **to experience your skills:** You have practiced your method and the whole team is fully briefed.

- **to have quality resources:** The church budget covers children's ministry and enables you to offer the best in all aspects of your program.

- **to have your prayers:** Leaders spend time praying regularly about children and know their situations.

- **to have your interest:** You remember previous conversations; you listen; you observe.

- **to be encouraged:** Time is given for thought when questions are posed, and answers are appropriately affirmed.

- **to know the boundaries:** It is clear what is expected of them, because a consistent approach is offered.

- **to be engaged:** Activities are designed with their abilities in mind, and a variety of approaches are used to ensure that all can participate.

- **to know, by your attitude, God's love:** You see them as precious, and understand that it is your privilege to be with them.

Pastoral Issues: Listening to Children _____

Listening is an important skill that needs constant practice. Listening is not waiting for your turn to speak; it is an activity in its own right.

Listed below are some things that help the listening process. Discuss them or, even better, role-play them and talk with your partner about how it felt to be listened to well and how it felt to be listened to badly.

Which of these pointers reminds you of something that has happened in your group? Which ones do you particularly need to remember? What's missing?

Language

1. Use language appropriate to the age of the children—neither too complex nor too simple.

2. Talk to children as you would to other adults; if you give them value and respect, they will reciprocate.

3. Never assume that you are all-knowing and that they are there to learn. It is more than likely that you will have a lot to learn from them.

4. Check that they understand what you say and are happy with it. Check with them that you have understood what they have been trying to say.

5. If you say something that is wrong, apologize.

Body Language

1. Be aware of your body language.
2. Come down to the children's level.
3. Do not use your physical size to intimidate them.
4. Use an open, positive stance—no closed positions, such as folded arms.
5. Maintain eye contact; if you are not looking at the child, you are not listening.

Use of Voice

1. Use a quiet voice: children will respond better to a softly spoken person than to one who shouts.
2. Be aware of local accents and phrases that you or they may not understand.
3. Remember that God has given us two ears and only one mouth—so we should listen more than we speak.

Pastoral Issues: Children Dealing with Loss

When there is a death, separation, divorce, or significant change or upheaval in the family, children have a right to pastoral care. Most children do not need therapeutic intervention in such circumstances. Like most of us, they simply need the loving attention of adults who are eager to connect with them, acknowl-edge what has happened, understand their pain and encourage the expression of feelings. All changes, large and small, carry with them a sense of loss, and children deserve to get whatever pastoral attention they need to cope with loss and grief.

Children's understanding of death depends upon their age, personality and life experience. Until the age of seven or so, they cannot fully grasp that death is permanent and they may believe that the dead person might return. Often, too, there is a fear that any other separation could be a forerunner of death. Small children are likely to feel frightened and insecure, voicing many questions over and over again. Reassurance and patience are needed in answering questions honestly, acknowledging that we don't know all the answers.

Most children over seven years of age understand that death is permanent and happens to everyone. They need to be reassured that they were not responsible for the death. Sometimes they even deny that it has happened. It is helpful for them to reminisce, maybe by looking at photographs and mementos.

Key points

- Remember that when a family is grieving, small acts of kindness mean a great deal.
- Acknowledge that children grieve.
- Children need to know that it is OK to have all sorts of strong feelings, and that these feelings might last for a while.
- Reassure children that they are in no way to blame for the loss.
- Give plenty of affection (as appropriate) to reassure children that they are cared about.
- Never assume that you know what they are feeling: ask them.
- Recognize children have pastoral care to offer as well as receive.

Share responses to this section, being sensitive to one another's experiences.

Being Safe

> You will need:
> ✔ Risk Assessment Recording Table, photocopied from page 87

Any premises in which an activity with children takes place should be physically safe and secure. It is the responsibility of your Christian community to ensure this, and one way of doing it is through risk assessments.

Risk assessments are a proactive approach to lessening the chance that an unexpected event will ever happen, and are used to identify possible problems and situations that could cause harm. They identify objects or activities that could cause harm and evaluate the associated risk, which is a combination of the likelihood of the hazard being realized and the severity of its outcome. Armed with this information, decisions can be made on how the risk is to be controlled.

Adopting a risk assessment approach for the premises in which you meet is good practice. It ensures that conditions are safe and that, so far as is reasonably practical, everything possible has been done to minimize the risk of danger. As a children's worker, you have a responsibility to be aware of what your Christian community has done in this area and, if possible, to review written documentation specific to your premises.

The Five Steps to Risk Assessment

1. **Identify the hazards:** What hazards could you envision in the place where you meet and work?
2. **Identify who might be harmed:** Who is at risk? Identify groups and types of people, not individuals.
3. **Identify existing controls:** What is in place to minimize the risk?
4. **Act:** Implement any further controls required and what needs to be updated or revised. What action needs to be taken to minimize the risks identified?
5. **Record your findings:** Who needs to be informed?

Take a walk through the training venue. Write down your findings on the risk assessment recording table, bearing in mind the perspective of a child, and then discuss the following questions.

- How safe is the physical environment in which your group meets? Make a special note of stairs, electrical outlets, doors, fire hazards, protruding nails, sharp corners, heaters, wooden floorboards, types and sizes of seating available, storage spaces and access.
- Spend time in the kitchen. What are the good points? What are the potential hazards? How hygienic is it?
- How accessible is the building for those with special physical needs?
- Do you think safety would be affected when the premises are busy?
- What are the security arrangements?
- What action needs to be taken to make your premises safer for children?

Remember also to do a risk assessment on the place where you normally work with children.

Biblical Thought

> You will need:
> ✔ Photographs of children (cut from newspapers and magazines) showing different ages/races/abilities, different contexts, different emotions and/or postcards collected from art galleries, commercial sets from publishers and greetings cards

Follow up the opening thought by passing around a selection of pictures of children. Reflect on them and how God loves us all without prejudice.

Children are offered as a model of God's being. Share the following biblical insights and/or participants' own suggestions.

- A child, Samuel, is the one who hears God speak and then shares a tough message with an adult who will not be glad to hear it (1 Samuel 3:1-18).

- A child, Miriam, spots an opportunity, copes in a sensitive way and changes history. Missing a child's contribution may mean missing a moment of enrichment in our relationship with God (Exodus 1:22–2:10).

As a group, recall moments when a child's insight enriched a group or individual.

Take the usual care needed when sharing personal observations and, if appropriate, discuss the requirements of sensitivity and confidentiality in talking about individual children.

Reflection on Learning

Adults are told to show Christ like attention to children by providing for their physical, spiritual and emotional needs: not offering a stone instead of bread; not placing stumbling blocks in their way; not provoking them by unreasonable behavior (Matthew 7:7-11; Mark 9:42; Ephesians 6:4).

- Share what you have learned from the session and what action you need to take.

- Identify the key people who have responsibility for your church or organization, and plan to ask them what they think about the pastoral awareness issues raised in this session.

Worship

God listens very carefully to what children say. In fact, God gives full attention to every word we all say. God loves you wholeheartedly and whatever is important to you is important to God.

In John 6:1–13, adults, children, and young people share together in feeding five thousand people, when the apparently minuscule and laughably ridiculous offering of a child contributes to the transformation of a difficult situation.

Prayer of St. Patrick's Breastplate

All: Christ be with me, Christ within me, Christ behind me, Christ before me, Christ beside me, Christ to win me, Christ to comfort and restore me, Christ beneath me, Christ above me, Christ in quiet, Christ in danger, Christ in hearts of all that love me, Christ in mouth of friend and stranger.

Leader: May Christ be in all our work with children, giving us wisdom to listen and eyes to see when something is wrong. Amen

Suggested Song

"Take this moment" (*Wild Goose Songs Vol. 3,* Wild Goose Publications)

Risk Assessment Recording Table

Name of Assessor _____

Date assessment carried out _____

Hazards	Who might be harmed	Existing controls	Action required	Action carried out by (signed and dated)

Reproduced with permission from *Equipped to Lead* published by Discipleship Resources © 2008

Personal Reflection Sheet

What did you learn from this session?

How will this affect the way you work with children?

What further items in this area would you like to follow up?

Reproduced with permission from *Equipped to Lead* published by Discipleship Resources © 2008

Portfolio Checklist

Learning Outcomes

⚙ To share insights about a variety of pastoral issues.

⚙ To explore how power is used in working with children.

⚙ To identify issues involved in providing a safe environment, physically, emotionally and spiritually, for children.

To show that the learning outcomes have been achieved, your portfolio must include at least the following. (Check when you have included each one in the file.)

☐ Personal Reflection Sheet

☐ Notes you have taken during Session 5, with any additional ideas

☐ A copy of your policy statement for child protection

☐ The completed worksheet on Safeguarding and Child Protection (see page 14)

☐ Completed Risk Assessment Recording Table

☐ A reflection about the building where you work with children

☐ Any other responses or reflections you wish to include

The participant's involvement in a group for Session 5, "Pastoral Awareness," is confirmed. The learning outcomes have been achieved through the evidence provided.

Signed (assessor) _____Date _____

Any comments from assessor

Signed (candidate) _____Date _____

Reproduced with permission from *Equipped to Lead* published by Discipleship Resources © 2008

SESSION SIX
Spirituality and the Bible

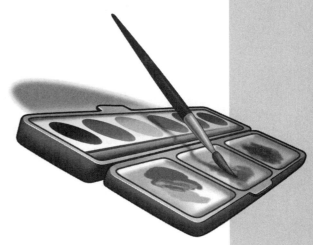

Aim

To explore the meaning of spirituality and its relationship with faith as expressed in the Bible.

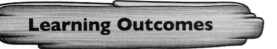
Learning Outcomes

- To explore the meaning of "spirituality" and its relationship with faith.
- To gain an understanding of ways in which the Bible can enrich prayer and spiritual activities.
- To experience a time of spiritual reflection.
- To develop an awareness of the different styles of prayer that may be used, both in community worship activities and in personal communication with God.

Materials Needed

Starters

✔ A flipchart and marker pens

Core

✔ Several photocopies (on card if possible) of the quotations from the writings of different faiths (see page 99). Cut each page into 14 individual cards, allowing one complete set of 14 cards for every two or three people.

✔ Bibles

✔ Four tables with a few chairs around them

✔ A copy of the four cards on the "Using the Bible Activity Sheet" (see page 100)

✔ At least four modern translations of the Bible (eight if possible)

✔ Plain paper, pencils, crayons

✔ A bowl or jar of assorted (threadable) beads (old necklaces from yard sales or second-hand shops are useful)

✔ Some balls of thin wool or thread

✔ Scissors

✔ Post-it® notes

✔ Four small cards, each with one of the following Bible references written on it: James 1:2–4; Romans 15:7; Colossians 1:9–14; Colossians 2:6–7

✔ A large, lighted candle (make sure it is safe)

✔ Enough tealights for everyone

Worship

✔ Copies of the Worship Activity Sheet pictures on page 101

✔ Some road maps, travel directions, guidebooks

✔ A Bible

✔ A flashlight

Opening Thought

One day Jesus was praying in a certain place. When he had finished, one of his disciples said to him, "Lord, teach us to pray, just as John taught his disciples." (Luke 11:1, GNB)

Defining Spirituality

> You will need:
> ✔ A flipchart and marker pens

At this stage, the focus is on spirituality and not on faith or religion. Religion helps us to make sense of our spirituality and is a result of our inherent desire to define something that we cannot explain.

Read the following aloud:

Spirituality is the sense that comes over us as we stare into the starlit sky, or watch the last fiery rays of an evening sunset. It is the morning shiver as we wake on a beautiful day and smell a richness in the air that we know and love from somewhere we can't quite recall. It is the mystery behind the beginning of time and beyond the limits of space. It is a sense of otherness that brings alive something deep in our hearts—Kent Nerburn, writer and theologian

Alternatively, write the following definitions on a flipchart and read them aloud:

Spirituality gives meaning to the material world, so that we may see it not as just matter and energy, but as a wonderful whole, perhaps part of a divine plan. — Liam Morland, Scout Movement, 2000

Spirituality is the part of the human heart that is in contact with the divine. —Dr. Rosemary Power, Ecumenical Development Officer, Swindon Unitary Authority, 2005

In groups of two or three, think of a time when you've been aware of something beyond your understanding or "outside yourself".

When and how have you experienced awe and wonder? As a whole group, explore how (or if) your individual experiences link with the above definitions of spirituality.

The Relationship of Spirituality and Faith

> You will need:
> ✔ Several photocopies (on cardstock if possible) of the quotations from the Writings of different faiths (see page 99). Cut each page into 14 individual cards, allowing one complete set of 14 cards for every two or three people.

Divide into groups of two or three, each having a set of the cards (well shuffled). Match up the quotations with the faiths from which they come. What are the similarities in the quotations? What are the differences? To what extent are spirituality and religion common to all times and all cultures?

Spirituality and the Bible

There are many ways of exploring the spirituality of the Bible. Usually, when we are with children, we tend to read or tell stories and ask the children to look for information, rather than help them to listen and find meanings for themselves in what they read. Reading or hearing scripture should be a spiritual experience, not just a fact-finding activity. It is one of the ways in which we can meet with God. The stories are important, but children also need to be given the freedom to think for themselves and relate what they hear to their own lives. They are the only ones who can do that. They are the real experts on their own lives and on their own relationship with God.

It is more helpful to discuss the stories with the children than simply to ask a range of "right or wrong" questions. This emphasizes the fact that we don't have the only answers, and that our relationship with the story is more important than factual recall. It is more important for children to hear the stories and respond than to remember the details. If they have experienced the story themselves in some way, they are more likely to remember it.

It is not helpful to tell the children what the story "means," or to impose one's own understanding of the story on them. As Jesus encouraged his listeners to discover their own understanding of his parables, so children's workers can allow their listeners to interpret stories in their own way.

In small groups, discuss how you feel about this attitude to using the Bible with children. Does it make you feel uneasy because you think you ought to have all the right answers? Or does it feel better to know that you are not expected to know everything? Do you feel comfortable with the idea that children can think things through with you? Do you think that you could learn anything from the children about the Bible stories you share with them?

How Many Ways Can You Tell a Bible Story? _____

> You will need:
> ✔ Bibles

In small groups, choose a Bible story and decide which of the following methods, suggested by a group of children's workers, you would use to tell the story to children.

- ⚙ Tell it from memory
- ⚙ Put it in your own words
- ⚙ Make a BIG picture (a mural, or life size)
- ⚙ Banners
- ⚙ Little pictures
- ⚙ Individual pictures
- ⚙ A video or film
- ⚙ Rap it
- ⚙ Ask people questions that will lead them to tell the story
- ⚙ Tell it with sound effects
- ⚙ Visual aids
- ⚙ Story coat (a coat with pictures and artifacts that tell or remind us of the story)
- ⚙ Audience participation
- ⚙ Masks
- ⚙ Cartoons
- ⚙ Songs (songs you know, or making up new words to old tunes, or old words to new tunes)
- ⚙ Puppets (stick, glove, marionettes, paper cut-outs, dancing dolls)
- ⚙ Read from the Dramatized Bible
- ⚙ Mime
- ⚙ Dance
- ⚙ Elaborate costume drama
- ⚙ Dressing-up box drama
- ⚙ Poetry
- ⚙ Improvise a drama
- ⚙ Narrator tells while actors act (or all do action)

Using the Bible

> You will need:
> - ✔ Four tables with a few chairs around them
> - ✔ A copy of the four cards on the "Using the Bible Activity Sheet" (see page 110)
> - ✔ At least four modern translations of the Bible (eight if possible)
> - ✔ Plain paper, pencils, crayons
> - ✔ A bowl or jar of assorted (threadable) beads
> - ✔ Some balls of thin wool or thread
> - ✔ Scissors
> - ✔ Post-it® notes
> - ✔ Four small cards, each with one of the following Bible references written on it: James 1:2-4; Romans 15:7; Colossians 1:9-14; Colossians 2:6-7
> - ✔ A large, lighted candle (make sure it is safe)
> - ✔ Enough tealights for everyone

Preparation

Set out the four tables (to be designated "Praise," "Letters," "Questions" and "Identity"), and some chairs, one table in each corner of the room. On each table, place one or two modern translations of the Bible, some plain paper, pencils, crayons and a copy of the appropriate card from the "Using the Bible Activity Sheet" on page 100.

On the "Praise" table, add the bowl or jar of beads, the balls of thin wool or thread, and scissors. Mark a psalm of praise in the Bible with a Post-it® note.

On the "Letters" table, add the four small cards showing the Bible references: James 1:2-4, Romans 15:7, Colossians 1:9-14 and Colossians 2:6-7.

On the "Questions" table, add the large, lighted candle (making sure it is safe) and enough tealights for everyone.

Nothing extra is required for the "Identity" table.

Method

Everyone is invited to visit each of the tables (in any order) and to follow the instructions on the cards. Each person makes his or her own journey round the room, moving from one table to the next when she or he is ready. Some people may prefer to do only one or two activities, while others may do them all. It doesn't matter. What is important is that each person is free to respond as she or he wishes. Play some quiet, restful music and place some chairs away from the tables in case anyone wants to be on his or her own for a while.

After 20 minutes, change the music to something that is a bit more lively. After a few more minutes, invite people to come and sit down in small groups and talk (if they wish) about the experiences they have had during this time of prayer and contemplation. Talk about the effect it had on them as individuals, being careful to take into account the fact that some people may have had deep feelings brought to the surface and may not be prepared to talk much about them.

Prayer

Prayer is an expression of spirituality, of making a relationship with the unknown. Christians focus their prayers on God through Jesus and, like spirituality itself, their prayers have many forms. Some people prefer formal prayers; others are happier with unspoken words. When we are working with children, it is possible that we will encourage them to use the prayer styles with which we are most comfortable, rather than helping them to discover other ways of communicating with God. Those ways might include:

- **Meditative prayer:** Reading a Bible verse or passage to help focus on God.
- **Liturgical prayer:** Repeating or reading a prayer that has been written or taught by someone else.
- **Active prayer:** Praying while walking or moving or doing something.
- **Shared prayers:** Praying aloud with others in small or large groups.
- **Conversational prayer:** Speaking to God in a conversational way, listening for answers as well as telling God our thoughts.
- **Spontaneous or "arrow" prayers:** An immediate response to something that is happening.

Can you remember your earliest prayers? Can you remember what you prayed about when you were young? If not, think of the first prayer you can remember praying. What sort of prayer was it? Look at the prayer styles below and try to identify what type of prayer you were praying.

Looking at the prayer styles, are there any that you prefer to use in private devotion? Which one(s)? Are there any that you find difficult to use?

Adoration

Adoration simply means "praise of God"; but is perhaps the hardest type of prayer. How do we mere human beings find words to tell God how wonderful he is? Adoration is entirely centred upon God. It is an opportunity to fasten all our attention on our trinitarian God alone, not on everything else around us (compare this with thanksgiving prayer).

Have you ever been in a situation where you have experienced awe and wonder—perhaps a scenic view or a piece of music or art? If you have had an experience like this, it will give you an insight into adoration. We want to share with God the feelings that arise

within us when we experience God's majesty and the mystery of his love.

Many of the Psalms can be used as prayers of adoration. As we look at them, we see how the psalmist was pouring out his sense of wonder to the God of Israel. Look at Psalms 8, 100, and 150 as examples.

Confession

When we become aware of being in the presence of God, we also become aware of all the inadequacies within us (sin): the wrong things that we have thought, said or done, and the good things we have neglected to do. All this can be quite overwhelming, and it is this confused and muddled situation that we bring to God in prayers of confession. We come before God and ask for forgiveness.

The downside of confession is that we can depress ourselves with our mistakes and faults, ending up in a situation where we feel far from God. Our God is a merciful God who does not condemn us but offers us pardon (through Christ's death and resurrection) and the opportunity of a new beginning, again and again, day after day and week after week. Look at biblical verses such as 1 John 1:9: "If we confess our sins, he is faithful and just and will forgive us our sins and purify us from all unrighteousness" (NIV).

Silence

Remember the saying, "God has given us two ears and one mouth, so we should listen twice as much as we speak." Taking time to listen to God is important but can be very difficult. We live in a world full of noise, so finding a place where we can be quiet and still, to meditate on him and hear his voice, is hard. But try; the results can be truly amazing!

Thanksgiving

Looking at the life of the world and our own lives, where can we see the power and grace of God at work? This is an opportunity to tell

God with pleasure. We know how to say "thank you" to friends, family and colleagues when they do something for us. Here we express our gratitude to God for all that he has done and is doing in the world and in our own lives. Examples are creation, Jesus' sacrifice, the gifts of the Holy Spirit, the Bible and so on.

It is important to think of both past and present in prayers of thanksgiving, as well as the future promise of life eternal. At different times of year, such as festival occasions, we may specify things that we want to say "thank you" for. For example, at Pentecost, we say "thank you" for the sending of the Holy Spirit.

Intercession

Intercessory prayer is an opportunity to pray for the people of God, to stand before God on behalf of the world and speak for it to him. It is very easy for our intercessions to become like a shopping list, as we think of all the places of the world we have heard about in the news, people we know who are ill or suffering, our family, friends and colleagues, and ourselves at the end—with a quick "Amen" before we rush off to the next thing.

Arrow prayers are another method of interceding for people or situations. Perhaps, when we hear an emergency siren, we can pray for the emergency service involved and for the situation they are heading toward. It is important to remember in our intercessions that we are not asking God to wave his magic wand and make all our wishes come true.

Now think of your work with children. Which style(s) of prayer do you use with children? Does it vary with the age of the children? Which style(s) of prayer do you encourage children to use? In small groups, select one prayer style and devise a prayer or activity that could be used with children.

Biblical Thought

Jesus often taught with stories and illustrations that left people to work out meanings for themselves. Maybe that would mean taking time to ponder alone or maybe talking it over with friends. New insights could dawn, or old things could be seen in new ways.

Once, Jesus asked the disciples whether they understood all the things he had been telling them. When they said "Yes," he went on to explain that becoming a disciple is like being "the owner of a house who brings out of his storeroom new treasures as well as old" (Matthew 13:51–52, NIV).

Reflection on Learning

Discuss the "Using the Bible" exercise, in which you visited different tables. Would it be helpful to use activity tables in this way when working with children? Have any of the group used ideas like this with children? Are any of the ideas useful? Could they be adapted to suit a particular group of children? Would it perhaps be best to use only one idea in a session with children, rather than a circuit of several tables?

Continue your thinking and discovery. The questions below can assist in the completion of a Personal Reflection Sheet for your portfolio.

- What encouragements, concerns and challenges has this module raised for you?
- What action will you take or encourage your church community to take as a result of this module?

- What will be the benefits for the children in your group and for your church community?
- Which aspects of this session can you talk about and check out with the children in your group?

Worship

> You will need:
> ✔ Copies of the "Worship Activity Sheet" pictures on page 101
> ✔ Some road maps, travel directions, guide books
> ✔ A Bible
> ✔ A flashlight

Place the maps, travel directions and flashlight on a central table where people can see and handle them. Display the pictures around the room. Encourage people to look at the pictures and the various items on the table. What can we see in the pictures? Does everyone see the same image? Can we all see two different images in each picture? Is one image more dominant than the other?

The Bible, in many ways, is like these pictures. Not everyone sees its message in the same way at the same time. When we ask God to help us as we read the Bible, we find in its words whatever is important for us at that moment. God's word is a lamp to guide us, not just a road map to follow without question, or the shortest route to a particular destination. It can shed light on our problems and help us to see our way through. It can point out the path we should take when we're uncertain about a decision we need to make.

Parables, in particular, can mean different things to different people. Read Luke 15:8-9 and reflect individually on its meaning. What is precious to you? How would you feel if you lost it? What would you do? Do you feel precious to God? What is God telling you about yourself, your life and your priorities in these words? Give the group a few minutes to think about these points and then have a time to share responses.

Prayers

The people who met Jesus on the way to Emmaus said to one another, "When he talked with us along the road and explained the Scriptures to us, didn't it warm our hearts?" (Luke 24:32).

Dear God, help us to burn with your light as we share your word with the children in our care. Amen.

Suggested Songs

"The word of the Lord is planted in my heart" (*Kidsource*, Kevin Mayhew)
"I want to walk with Jesus Christ" (*Mission Praise*, Marshall Pickering)

Spiritual Writings

You are a sun; you are a full moon. You are light upon light. You are an elixir, very precious. You light up our hearts.	*Sufi poet, Islam*
I have transcended Time and Space. I shall never be born again. I am smaller than an atom. Yet have I expanded beyond Space itself.	*Gyanba Tukaram, Hindu saint*
Deep within the self is the light of God. It radiates through the expanse of his creation.	*Guru Amar Das, Majh, Sikh*
Infinite Being is the all-encompassing consciousness from which the universe was created.	*New Age spiritual insight*
The Word was the source of life, and this life brought light to people.	*Gospel of John, Christianity*
He who having been heedless is heedless no more, illuminates this world like the moon freed from clouds.	*Dhammapada 13, Buddhism*
You are the source of all life, and because of your light we see the light.	*Tehillim 36:9, Judaism*

Reproduced with permission from *Equipped to Lead* published by Discipleship Resources © 2008

Praise

Read the psalm marked in the Bible, and think about all the things the writer is thanking God for. Are they things that make you want to praise God? What would you like to thank God for?

Think about all the things in your life that remind you of God's love for you. Thread a bead on to the wool for each of these things. Perhaps you could choose a bead that reminds you in some way of the thing you are saying "thank you" for. While you thread the beads, thank God for all these blessings. Take the beads home as a reminder.

Questions

Think of some of the parts of the Bible that you find difficult. They may be difficult because they are hard to understand or because they say things that we don't really want to hear. Sometimes, passages in the Bible seem to ask us more questions than they give us answers. Think of something that puzzles you about what the Bible says, and concentrate on this issue. Ask God to help you to understand, or to accept, this message. Remember that you may not know the answer or explanation for a very long time, but this will be OK. We have a whole lifetime in which to learn.

Light a tealight from the larger candle and, as you do so, ask God to reveal to you the answer at the right time (which may not be now).

Letters

Choose one of the Bible references and find the verses in a Bible. They are all taken from the letters written to the new churches soon after Jesus' life on earth. The writer (Paul or James) is helping the new churches to live out their faith and to be good witnesses to the difference that Jesus has made to their lives. He is encouraging to the new Christians, but he is honest as well, and sometimes sounds quite severe.

Imagine he has written these words to you and your church. Read the passage and think about how it might relate to you. What is God saying to you through this letter? If you would like to, write a quick note to Paul or James in reply.

Identity

Think of your favorite story about Jesus. Imagine yourself there in the scene while it is happening. In your imagination, let the story unfold as if you were watching a movie. What can you see, hear, smell or touch? Who else is there? What emotions are you experiencing?

If you would like to, draw a picture of the scene with you in it, while you are thinking. How do you feel? What can you hear Jesus saying to you?

Worship Activity Sheet

How many legs on the elephant?

A bird or a rabbit?

A vase or two faces?

The front or back of a book?

Elegant lady or elderly woman?

Lady or saxophonist?

Personal Reflection Sheet

What did you learn from this session?

How will this affect the way you work with children?

What further items in this area would you like to follow up?

Portfolio Checklist

Learning Outcomes

⚙ To explore the meaning of "spirituality" and its relationship with faith.

⚙ To gain an understanding of ways in which the Bible can enrich prayer and spiritual activities.

⚙ To experience a time of spiritual reflection.

⚙ To develop an awareness of the different styles of prayer that may be used, both in community worship activities and personal communication with God.

To show that the learning outcomes have been achieved, your portfolio must include at least the following. (Check when you have included each one in the file.)

☐ Personal reflection sheet

☐ Notes from the starter activity

☐ Your views on using Bible stories with children

☐ A record of how you might tell Bible stories to children in a variety of ways

☐ Examples of how you have prayed with children in two different ways

☐ A brief account of a personal experience of spiritual reflection

☐ Any other responses or reflections you wish to include

The participant's involvement in a group for Session 6, "Spirituality and the Bible," is confirmed. The learning outcomes have been achieved through the evidence provided.

Signed (assessor) _____ Date _____

Any comments from assessor

Signed (candidate) _____ Date _____

Reproduced with permission from *Equipped to Lead* published by Discipleship Resources © 2008

Equipped to Lead
Children's Sunday School Guide

Certificate

This is to certify that

_____

has completed

*Equipped to Lead*_____

at_____

Signed _____(trainer)

Name _____

Date _____

Notes

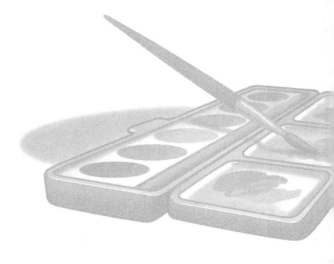

Notes

Notes

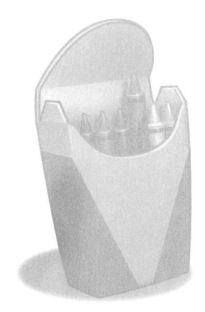

Notes

Notes

Notes

Notes

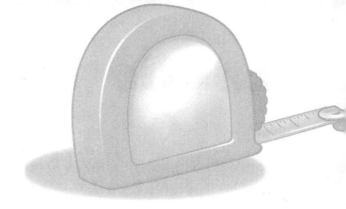

Bibliography

Simon Bass. *Special Children Special Needs*. CHP, 2003.

Jerome Berryman. *Godly Play*. Augsburg Press, 1991.

John Bradford. *Caring for the Whole Child*. The Children's Society, 1995.

Francis Bridger. *Children Finding Faith*. SU, 2000.

Marcia Bunge. *The Child in Christian Thought*. Eerdmans, 2001.

Charter for Children in the Church. URC, 2004.

Robert Coles. *The Spiritual Life of Children*. Harper Collins, 1992.

Consultative Group on Ministry among Children. *The Child in the Church*. British Council of Churches, 1976.

————. *Unfinished Business*, CCBI, 1991.

Kathryn Copsey. *From the Ground Up*. BRF, 2005.

Wendy Duffy. *Children and Bereavement*. CHP, 2003.

Janet Marshall Eibner and Susan Graham Walker. *God, Kids and Us*. Morehouse, 1997.

Caroline S. Fairless. *Children at Worship*. Congregations in Bloom, Church Publishing Inc., 2000.

James Fowler. *Stages of Faith*. Harper Collins, 1995.

Leslie Francis. *Urban Hope and Spiritual Health*. Epworth, 2006.

General Synod Board of Education. *Children in the Way*. CHP, 1988.

————. *How Faith Grows*. National Society/Chirch House Publishing, 1991.

————. *Sharing the Good News with Children*, CHP, 2003.

David Hay and Rebecca Nye. *The Spirit of the Child*. Jessica Kingsley Publishers, 2006.

John Henson. *Good as New: A Radical Retelling of the Scriptures*. O Books, 2004.

Craig Jutila. *Leadership Essentials for Children's Ministry*. Group Publishing, 2002.

Light. Bible-based learning resources for all ages, SU.

Kathleen Marshall and Paul Parvis. *Honouring Children*. St Andrews Press, 2004.

David Ng and Virginia Thomas. *Children in the Worshipping Community*. John Knox Press, 1981.

Betty Pedley and John Muir. *Children in the Church?* CHP, 1997.

Roots for Churches: Worship and Learning for the Whole Church. MPH, bi-monthly.

Claire Saunders and Hilary Porritt. *Working with 8–10s*. SU, 2005.

Catherine Stonehouse. *Joining Children on the Spiritual Journey*. Baker Books, 1998.

Hans-Ruedi Weber. *Jesus and the Children*. WCC, 1979.

Wholly Worship Too. URC, 2000.

Judith Wigley. *Working with Under 5s*. SU, 2005.

Tricia Williams and John Stephenson. *Working with 11–14s*. SU, 2005.

Margaret Withers. *Fired Up . . . Not Burnt Out*. BRF, 2001.

————. *Where Are the Children?* BRF, 2005.

Gretchen Wolff Pritchard. *Offering the Gospel to Children*. Cowley, 1992.

Michael Yaconelli. *Dangerous Wonder*. Navpress, 1998.